Scottish Lighthouses

Sharma Krauskopf

Appletree Press

The Globe Pequot Press

Published by:

The Appletree Press Ltd
The Old Potato Station
14 Howard Street South
Belfast BT7 1AP
Tel: +44 (0) 28 90 243074
Fax: +44 (0) 28 90 246756
E-mail: reception@appletree.ie
Web Site: www.appletree.ie

The Globe Pequot Press
246 Goose Lane
Guilford, Connecticut 06437
USA

Scottish Lighthouses

Library of Congress
Cataloging-in-Publication
data is available.

ISBN 0-7627-0943-X

The publisher wishes to thank:

Jim Bain for permission to publish photographs on the front cover, pages 6, 10, 22, 30, 31, 32, 33, 34, 35, 36, 78 and 79

Charles Tait for permission to publish photographs on pages 9, 13, 14, 17, 18, 25, 26, 28 lower, 29, 39, 40, 42, 43, 44-45, 46, 47, 48-49, 53, 54, 55, 57, 58, 59, 60, 61, 62, 63, 64, 65, 66-67, 68, 69, 70, 71, 73, 74, 7 and 77 lower

Genevieve Leaper for permission to publish photographs on pages 21, 50, 51, 52 lower, 76, 77 upper, 80, 81 and 82

The Museum of Scottish Lighthouses, Fraserburgh for permission to publish photographs on pages 27, 28, 37 and 52 upper

Books by Sharma Krauskopf
Scotland – The Complete Guide
The Last Lighthouse

For children:
Moonbeam Cow

This book is dedicated to Rob Blackwell of Appletree Press whose love of lighthouses made it possible.

Contents

Introduction   6

  Why Lighthouses?   6

    The Country of Scotland   8

    The Northern Lighthouse Board   12

    The Stevenson Family   19

    The Tour   24

Thirty-one Scottish Lights   26

  Southern Scotland   26

    Turnberry   26

    Corsewall Point   27

    Mull of Galloway   29

    Mull of Kintyre   30

    Sanda   32

  Hebrides   35

    Rinns of Islay   35

    Skerryvore   37

    Hyskeir   38

    Neist Point   40

    Isle of Ornsay   41

    Butt of Lewis   44

    Flannan Isle   46

  West Coast   50

    Ardnamurchan   50

    Stoer Head   52

    Rubh' Re   53

    Cape Wrath   54

North Coast   56

    Dunnet Head   56

    Holburn Head   58

    Pentland Skerries   61

Orkney   63

    North Ronaldsay   63

    Noup Head   64

    Hoy High and Hoy Low   67

Shetland   69

    Muckle Flugga   69

    Eshaness   72

    Sumburgh   74

    Fair Isle North and Fair Isle South   76

East Coast   78

    Bell Rock   78

    Bass Rock   80

    Buchan Ness   82

Glossary   84

Bibliography   88

Index   89

Map   96

INTRODUCTION

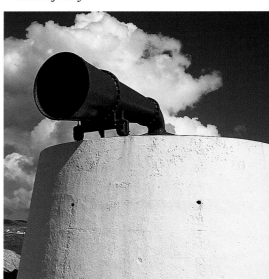

Pharos Loquitur

Far in the bosom of the deep,
O'er these wild shelves my watch I keep;
A ruddy gem of changeful light,
Bound on the dusky brow of night,
The seaman bids my lustre hail,
And scorns to strike his timorous sail.

Sir Walter Scott on his visit to Bell Rock on 30 July 1814

Standing alone on a rock far above the sea the kilted bagpiper gazes at a beautiful white lighthouse trimmed in black and gold. The mellow sound of the pipes echoes over the heather-covered hills as the mist creeps across the sea. So goes a romantic postcard description of a Scottish lighthouse. A few years ago I bought a postcard exactly like this of the Mull of Kintyre. Looking back now I realise how misleading that postcard was.

It is my hope that through this book I can draw another picture which gives a more realistic portrait of Scotland's lighthouses. Scotland has an important place in the history of the lighthouses of the world and in this introduction we will look at the country of Scotland, the Northern Lighthouse Board – the controlling body for the Scottish lighthouses – and the famous Stevenson family of lighthouse engineers who designed many of the Scottish lights. With this information in hand we can set sail on a tour of some of my favourite Scottish lighthouses.

Why Lighthouses?

I am often asked why I choose to live at a remote lighthouse station on the Shetland Islands. I attempted to answer this question in an article I wrote for Rob Blackwell to whom this book is dedicated. (*Lighthouse Digest* later published the article.) Here is what I said:

Not often do I stop to measure why something matters in my life unless someone asks or something brings it to my attention. Recently an email slipped into my list with the title "Lighthouse". Almost compulsive about answering my email, especially those with the title "Lighthouse", I read it at once. It was from a reader in Ireland who loves lighthouses.

He asked me the question, "Why lighthouses?" I wanted to flippantly declare "Why not?", except the writer is a lighthouse aficionado searching for an explanation for his fascination as well as my own. In my usual hasty email style I dashed off as an answer a list of words which I associate with lighthouses. The question haunted me and to preserve my sanity it merited a complete answer. So here, Rob, and all of the other lighthouse lovers who might read this, is a more comprehensive answer.

Firstly, lighthouses are ordinarily found in remote areas with a small number of human neighbours. At Neist Point, which I have visited many times, the nearest human beings are a 45-

minute walk away! For most Scottish lighthouses the only next-door neighbours are sheep and as many lighthouses can only be approached by boat, I guess their neighbours are fish. So my first reason, not necessarily the most important, is their remote location where I can be completely alone. That is a necessity, since my life is hectic, full of deadlines and chaos. I have a compulsion to be surrounded by nature in isolation where I can think and feel nothing if I like.

Secondly, all of the stations' postal addresses could be "Ocean Place". Their relationship with the sea is an intimate one. Some are found on peninsulas surrounded on three sides by water. Others, from on top of lofty heads, view miles of ocean. "Flat land lights" are situated where one can walk out the door and within a few feet be on the shore. Rock stations are usually the only buildings on small islands where access is by boat. The air surrounding a lighthouse is fresh with the smell of the sea. The melody of the waves touching the shore is often the only sound you hear. Like classical music this melody can be violent and loud or soft and peaceful. A valid reason for someone like me who lives on a farm surrounded by pastures is they are a stone's throw from the ocean. Our farm is beautiful but I continually yearn for the sea.

If you are a nature lover then a lighthouse is the best place in the world to see ocean creatures in their natural environment. I have seen dolphins, whales, seals and many different types of seabirds including puffins within a short distance of many keepers' houses. My favourites are the seals, which at most Scottish lighthouses can be seen through the windows playing outside on the rocks. Good fishing is a few feet beyond the house and there is nothing better than a lobster you have caught over the side of the lighthouse wall. Being close enough to a whale to hear the blow is sufficient reason for me to love all lighthouses.

Lighthouses are a part of history, some dating back to the 1700s. If the towers could talk, they would relate an extraordinary saga of man and his ongoing relationship with the sea. They could tell of tragedy and triumph that have occurred in the world of water which surrounds them. Staggering tales of the courageous and devoted keepers who kept the lights blazing or tragic stories of death and shipwrecks are forever chiselled in their hard stone exterior. Most of the lighthouses are historic buildings.

Many lighthouse buildings are physically beautiful. Set in exquisite locations, the nature of their architecture leads to feelings of majesty. The tall towers stretch out to touch the sky while brilliant beacons pierce the black of night. During the day even the Fresnel lens looks like magnificent gold diamonds sitting in their towers with the light streaming through them to paint rainbows of colour on the ground below. For many lighthouse buffs beauty is the main reason they cherish these structures.

Lighthouses, due to changes in technology, have in many places become unnecessary. They have gone from being lovingly tended by their keepers to the cold reality of being operated by machines through phone lines. Thank goodness, in Scotland the lights are still shining and the buildings maintained. In many parts of the world the lights have been shut off and the properties abandoned. In the state where I lived in America we once had 247 lighthouses on the Great Lakes but now we have less than 100 in good condition. They have been allowed to decay and deteriorate. Tears come to my eyes when I think of something so historic and beautiful as Scotland's Duncansby Head being allowed to die a slow and hideous death. At least I know the Northern Lighthouse Board will not allow that to happen to Duncansby. If the property cannot be saved, they will destroy it quickly and finally. I relate this to how I feel when I know a good friend might die and the time we have left becomes so very valuable.

Having now given you some of the intellectual reasons, I want to close with an emotional moment in my life which puts it together.

Snow is gently falling as we drive to the lonely peaceful car park a few hundred feet from Corsewall Light. Having had dinner with Tom Kelly, the occasional keeper for Corsewall, we were on our way to his house for a cup of tea but had made a short detour wanting to see the lighthouse in night operation up close. Walking to a rocky viewpoint where the only sound was the crashing mad and angry sea below us, we looked back at the lighthouse. The beacon striking out from the tower was revolving in the snow. The light made long rays of silver narrow at the beginning and wider the further from the tower they penetrated the sky. Framed in the beam of light was the glitter of hundreds of twinkling speckles caused by the ice crystals in the snow. I once related this scene in another of my published stories to the blades of a helicopter revolving in the night.

As I wrote this article I remembered that night and realised that for me it answered the question "Why Lighthouses?" The beacon illuminating the snow was alone in the sky, continuing to keep ships safe, creating another moment of history among the hundreds of such moments since the lighthouse was built. Surrounded by the sounds of the sea that instant belonged only to the four of us. Each of us got back in the car with snowflakes mixing with our tears of wonderment accompanied with a deep feeling of total serenity. That is the best answer I can think of to "Why Lighthouses?" and its memory will stay with me forever.

THE COUNTRY OF SCOTLAND

Scotland is a land of magnificent beauty wrapped in a package for all to enjoy. The country is 275 miles long and 150 miles wide and has only 5.2 million people within its 30,414 square miles. The capital is Edinburgh, which has a population of 420,000 and is the seat of the Scottish Democratic Parliament. Scotland is part of the United Kingdom and as such the Head of State is Queen Elizabeth II. The people are descended from the Celts, Anglo-Saxons, Scots and Picts. The country's official language is English but the native languages of Gaelic and Scots are still spoken. The main religion is Christianity, represented chiefly by the Presbyterian, Anglican and Roman Catholic denominations.

Scotland echoes with the cries of a long complex history, since the country has been a battleground for most of its existence. From the north came the Vikings, from the south stormed the English, and from inside its own borders proud clans fought each other over territorial lines and power. But these conflicts are part of the appeal of the country. A plaid-garbed Highlander running through the mist to slay the invading southerner is a familiar image, which created great films like *Rob Roy* and *Braveheart*. Ancient ruins, some over five thousand years old, speak to the mysterious people who created them. The physical beauty of the land counteracts the violence of the battles. Heather-covered hills, gently touched with a grey sweeping mist, and gleaming lochs generate romance as performed in the ever-popular musical "Brigadoon" and its songs.

There are few parts of the world that hold such enchantment and mystery as the seas around Scotland. The country has six thousand miles of awe-inspiring coastline (69 per cent

North Ronaldsay

of the total United Kingdom coastline) and possesses a spectacular collection of over eight hundred islands, mountains, rocks and stacks surround Scotland's shores. The mountains reach down to touch the sea creating magnificent seascapes. Another enchanting thing about Scotland is with all the focus on its history, the modern country has its own charm. The physical beauty has not changed and good roads and exceptional public transport make it easy to reach the most spectacular of the sights within a day or two. Historic places are well marked and tourist boards can point you in the right direction to see the best of each region.

The geography and geology are complex and every region has a distinct personality; travelling a few short miles, one can find remarkable differences. In discussing the lighthouses covered in this book we will be dropping in on some of those extremely different physical environments.

"Varied" describes Scotland's climate perfectly. There are wide differences in climate over small distances and it is quite common to get two seasons or more in one day. Warmth can be followed by rain, sleet and even snow. Even though Scotland is far north, the Gulf Stream keeps the temperature mild (well, relatively mild). The Highlands, however, can have severe weather at any time. The east coast has a tendency to be cool and dry with winter temperatures rarely dropping below freezing, but the wind-chill temperature can be incredibly cold because of the bone-chilling currents of air off the North Sea. The west coast is milder and wetter, with average summer highs of 19°C (66°F). May and June are the driest months with July and August the warmest. In the north the sun barely sets in summer, while in winter it hardly rises.

SOUTHERN SCOTLAND

Included in our section on Southern Scotland are lighthouses in the areas of Ayrshire, Galloway and Kintyre. Most visitors think of only the Highlands and miss the beautiful southern part of the country. Southern Scotland contains blue-coloured rolling hills permeated with the tales and relics of hundreds of battles between the Scots and their always aggressive English neighbours. The area is packed with stately homes and fortified castles and is alive with history, being the homeland of famous historical characters such as Robert Burns, Sir Walter Scott and Robert the Bruce.

Ayrshire, the land of Robert Burns, is an area of contrast between the flat mainland and islands, while Galloway has lonely hills with dark woods leading to rich farmlands and a sunny south-facing coast. The towns have great character and include some eye-catching pastel-painted houses along wide main streets. The lovely southern coastline is made warmer by the North Atlantic Drift (Scotland's part of the Gulf Stream) and has palm trees growing near the sea – it is blessed with lots of gardens to visit. Coastal farms have fields that run down to the sea, and it is common to see cows and sheep grazing near the shoreline.

The long narrow peninsula of Kintyre has superb views across to the islands of Gigha, Islay and Jura, and the 9-mile Crimean Canal that opened in 1801 almost cuts the peninsula in half. The canal is a delightful inland waterway and its 15 locks bustle with pleasure craft in the summer. The town of Tarbert (meaning "isthmus" in Gaelic) takes its name from the fact it is narrow enough to drag a boat across between Loch Fyne and West Loch. The Viking King Magnus Barfud, who in 1198 was granted by treaty as much land as he could sail around, first accomplished this feat.

Sanda

Further south beyond Campbeltown the road ends at the headland known as the Mull of Kintyre made famous when former Beatle Paul McCartney commercialised a traditional pipe tune of the same name. Robert the Bruce learned patience in his constant struggles with the English by observing a spider weaving an elaborate web in his cave on Rathlin Island, west of Kintyre. We will visit five lighthouses in this area – Corsewall Point near Stranraer; Turnberry, the home of the famous golf course; the Mull of Galloway on the south-western tip of Scotland; Sanda on the south and the Mull of Kintyre on the west of the Kintyre Peninsula.

HEBRIDES

Of the eight hundred islands the largest group is the Hebrides with five hundred islands lying off the west coast of mainland Scotland. The Inner Hebrides includes such beautiful places as Skye, Mull, Iona and Jura. A body of water called the Little Minch separates this group of islands from the Outer Hebrides. The first group of lighthouses is in the Inner Hebrides area. Hyskeir, an island near the beautiful green island of sparsely populated Rhum, can only be reached by boat. Skerryvore lies off the Isle of Tiree. Tiree is a low fertile island, with more sunshine than the rest of Britain. Being 60 per cent shell sand no trees can grow on Tiree but crofts prosper.

Skye offers some of Scotland's most dramatic scenery including the Cuillin Hills. It is a land of contrast as can be seen by the two lighthouses we will visit – Neist Point and the Isle of Ornsay. The Butt of Lewis and Flannan Isle are located in the Outer Hebrides, often called the Western Isles, an archipelago stretching 140 miles from the Butt of Lewis to Barra Head. The western edge of Scotland, the Outer Hebrides is made up of some of the oldest rock on earth. Miles of sandy beaches often edge the western coasts of the islands while the eastern shores are composed mostly of peat bogs that the islanders use for fuel. The islands show evidence of inhabitation for the last 6,000 years and Gaelic is still spoken. Islay is world renowned for its single malt whiskies.

WEST COAST

Many consider the north-western coast the most beautiful part of Scotland with lofty mountains converging on the sea. The area is dotted with numerous peninsulas, big headlands, sea stacks, narrow sea lochs and interesting bays. Access to the area can be difficult with many one-track roads. Inadequate access restrains population growth so the area has a feeling of isolation. I have picked four lighthouses in this area beginning with Ardnamurchan on the remote peninsula of the same name. The Ardnamurchan peninsula has some of the west coast's best-kept secrets with a sinuous coastline, rocky mountains and beaches. Some of the best beaches are found on the tip of the peninsula, the most westerly point of mainland Scotland. Lighthouses of Stoer Head, Rubh' Re and Cape Wrath are farther north on the west coast of Sutherland. North-west Sutherland owes most of its beauty to its mountains. Unencumbered by connected ranges, mountains stand in lonely splendour pushing skyward from a base of lochs and lochans, edged by a striking coastline of cliffs and sea lochs. The area is rich in wildlife and flowers.

NORTH COAST

All of our lighthouses in the north coast area lie in Caithness. This county is in the north-east of Scotland, bounded on the north by the Pentland Firth, on the east and south-east by the North Sea, and on the west and south-west by the county of Sutherland. Caithness is about 43 miles in length and 30 miles in breadth comprising an area of 618 square miles. Tourists do not often visit the region because on a map it looks quite a distance from the urban and more frequented areas, but maps can be deceiving and it is easy to travel there. Caithness consists of green rolling farmland which, being so far north, surprises the traveller. Thurso has approximately 9,000 residents, which makes it the largest town in Caithness. It is situated on the shallow braes to either side of the River Thurso valley. Two lighthouses on our tour, Holburn Head and Dunnet Head, are near Thurso – Dunnet Head is the most northerly point on the Scottish mainland. Separating the north-east tip of the mainland from Orkney, the Pentland Firth links the North Sea and the Atlantic Ocean in an incomprehensible turmoil of swirling eddies, tide races, counter currents and whirlpools. The Pentland Skerries Lighthouse is located at the eastern end of the Pentland Firth.

ORKNEY AND SHETLAND

North of the mainland of Scotland, stretching nearly 150 miles into the North Sea, are the twin archipelagos of Orkney and Shetland. Both groups of islands are exposed to frequent and long storms from all directions. The Orkney Islands archipelago is made up of 67 islands; however, the 19,000 people who live in the Orkneys inhabit less than 30 of these. Rich Norse-sounding place names indicate the closeness of the islands to the Viking era. The Orkneyinga Sagas, the tales of the Viking occupation, tell about the long history of the islands – the Orkneys have the greatest concentration of prehistoric relics found anywhere in Western Europe. Farming is extensive and first-time visitors are surprised by a pastoral landscape of green fields in summer and the golden fields of autumn. The island cliffs are home to thousands of seabirds and it is common to see seals and otters playing among the rocks on the shores. I have information on four Orkney lighthouses – North Ronaldsay at the far north of the group on the island of the same name, Noup Head located on the island of Westray, and Hoy High and Hoy Low on the island of Graemsay.

The northernmost outpost of Scotland, the Shetland Islands, is a group of 100 islands of which only 20 are inhabited, and which is closer to Norway than mainland Scotland. Nowhere in the Shetlands is more than 5 miles from the sea thanks to the voes and smaller geos – the long fingers of the sea that find their way inland. With all of these bodies of water reaching inward, the Shetlands have 900 miles of coastline. Crofts and small fields with virtually no trees make up most of the landscape. With a population of only 27,000, the islands have wild beauty, solitude and empty spaces. In spite of the island's northern location the winters are only slightly colder here than on the mainland because of the North Atlantic Drift. Summers are cool but a visit is worthwhile to experience the summer gloaming where the days never seem to end. Winds can be strong but rainfall is less than in many areas in mainland Britain. You will find five lighthouses from the Shetland Islands in this book. Muckle Flugga on the most northerly point in Shetland, Eshaness on the wild west coast of the main island, Sumburgh Head on the southern tip of the main island and Fair Isle North and South located on Fair Isle halfway between the Shetland and the Orkney group.

EAST COAST

The east coast of Scotland is more heavily populated and includes the capital, Edinburgh. It is a mixture of flat coastline with beautiful beaches and some mountains. It is known for its famous golf courses close by the sea. The further north you go on the east coast the less populated it becomes. From this area I have selected the Bell Rock, Bass Rock and Buchan Ness lighthouses.

THE NORTHERN LIGHTHOUSE BOARD

Since the early Vikings and Celts many inhabitants of Scotland were fishermen and sea traders which helped them to survive their constant battles with England. Navigational assistance was essential to reduce the number of shipwrecks and the loss of life. Not until the early 1600s – with the expansion of coal-mining, salt-making and fishing – was any movement made to create some type of warning device for ships. There was resistance at first from Scottish shipowners and merchants since they would have to pay the heavy tolls that would be charged for any navigational aids. But the seas were growing busier, the danger remained and the discussion continued. Finally, in 1636, the Isle of May Old Light was built. Three men, James Maxwell of Innerwick, Alexander Cunningham of Barns and his son, John the "fiar" of Barns, were given the right to build a "convenient" lighthouse on the highest point on the Isle of May. A 25-foot square tower 40 feet tall was built. The lower half of the original tower still stands. The light was a coal fire burned in a brazier mounted on the top of the building.

After the Isle of May Light, local bodies around the estuaries of the Tay, the Solway and the Clyde became interested in making their stretch of coastline safer. In 1687 the seamen of Dundee established "leading" coal lights to show the way through the sandbanks at the entrance to the Tay. In April 1756 the world's first public authority with lighthouse management as its chief function was established in Scotland and a lighthouse was to be built on the Little Cumbrae making navigation in the Firth and River of Clyde more extensive and safer. The lighthouse was a 28-feet-high circular stone tower with an inside stair leading to the "altar" on top which had a grate for a coal fire.

An almost uninterrupted succession of storms, unequalled in history, struck the British coasts in 1782. Following concern caused by these storms, and led by a determined local MP, George Dempster of Dunnichen in Angus, Parliament passed an important piece of legislation on 27 June 1786: "An Act for erecting certain Lighthouses in the Northern Parts of Great Britain" in order, as the preamble stated, to

Eshaness

"…conduce greatly to the security navigation and the fisheries." In addition it stipulated the building of four lights – these were Kinnaird Head, North Ronaldsay, Mull of Kintyre and Eilean Glas. The Act established the amount that ships would be charged for using the four lights once they were operating. The charge was one penny per ton on British ships and two pennies per ton on foreign vessels passing any of the lights except whaling fleets and ships making the Archangel and White Sea run.

The Act established an independent board of trustees and commissioners; thus, the Northern Lighthouse Board was born. It is believed this was the first group in the world established for the only purpose of managing a number of lighthouses on a countrywide basis. The Board was composed of two Crown Officers for Scotland, the Lord Advocate and Solicitor General, the Lord Provosts and first Bailies of Edinburgh and Glasgow, the Provosts of Aberdeen, Inverness and Campbeltown, and the Sheriffs of certain maritime areas – Edinburgh, Lanark, Renfrew, Bute, Argyll, Inverness, Ross, Orkney, Caithness and Aberdeen.

They met for the first time on 1 August 1786. Since they could not assess duty until the four lights were built, they set about borrowing the needed funds to build the lights from five burghs. They hired Thomas Smith, a light-maker who had constructed a lighting device with an Argand glass chimney and a parabolic reflector to increase its luminosity, as the first engineer. More about him when we discuss the Stevenson family.

Many changes have taken place since the Northern Lighthouse Board was created. The Isle of Man authorities wanted a Stevenson to engineer their lights so the Isle of Man lights became the responsibility of the Northern Lighthouse Board in 1815. In 1836, under the United Kingdom Lighthouse Act, Trinity House was given supervision over the Northern Lighthouse Board and the Commissioners for Irish Lights.

Currently, the Northern Lighthouse Board consists of the Lord Advocate, the Solicitor General, the Sheriffs, the Principal of Scotland, the Lord Provosts of Edinburgh,

Glasgow and Aberdeen, the Provost of Inverness, the Convenor of the Council for Argyll and Bute, a nominee from the Isle of Man and a five-member Board serving a term of three years, elected by the Commissioners. The Chairman, elected by his peers, usually serves for a period of two years, but with the option of remaining in office for a third year.

The Commissioners of Northern Lighthouses manage all lighthouses, buoys and beacons throughout Scotland and its adjoining seas and islands, including the Isle of Man, under Section 195 of the Merchant Shipping Act of 1995. This includes 84 major automatic lighthouses, 116 minor lights, 117 buoys, 43 unlit beacons, 23 racon stations, 19 fog stations and 3 DGPS stations. The corporate body is still known as the Northern Lighthouse Board (the Board), constituted by Section 193 of that Act. Under Section 197 of the 1995 Act as amended, the Commissioners have various powers and responsibilities dealing with the provision, maintenance, alteration, inspection and control of lighthouses, buoys and beacons. Section 253 of the Act gave them wreck removal powers. The Merchant Shipping and Maritime Security Act 1997 gives the Board the additional authority to contract with third parties, utilising spare capacity, with the permission of the Secretary of State. Operational costs are met from a "General Lighthouse Fund" financed by the collection of Light Dues paid by commercial ships and by fishing vessels over 33 feet in length calling at ports in their jurisdiction. The powers and duties

Noup Head

are stipulated in the Merchant Shipping Act of 1894.

Since its inception the Northern Lighthouse Board has built and managed the following major lights. All lights are still functioning unless otherwise indicated.

Date Built

1787 – Kinnaird Head on the east coast of Scotland was automated in 1991
1787 – Mull of Kintyre in south-west Scotland was automated in 1996
1789 – North Ronaldsay in the Orkney Islands was discontinued in 1809
1789 – Eilean Glas on the Isle of Scalpay in the Outer Hebrides was automated in 1978
1790 – Pladda off the south end of the Isle of Mull was automated in 1990
1794 – Pentland Skerries at the east end of Pentland Firth was automated in 1994
1804 – Inchkeith on the Firth of Forth was automated in 1986
1806 – Start Point on the island of Sanday in the Orkney Islands was automated in 1962

1811 – Bell Rock in the North Sea off the east coast of Scotland was automated in 1988

1816 – Isle of May in the centre of the Firth of Forth was automated in 1989

1816 – Coreswall Point on the south-west coast of the mainland was automated in 1994

1818 – Point of Ayre on the Isle of Man was automated in 1991

1818 – Calf of Man off the Isle of Man was discontinued in1875

1821 – Sumburgh Head on the southern end of mainland Shetland was automated in 1991

1825 – Rinns of Islay on the south-east tip of the Inner Hebridean island of Islay was automated in 1998

1827 – Buchan Ness on the east coast of mainland Scotland was automated in 1988

1828 – Cape Wrath on the north-west corner of mainland Scotland was automated in 1998

1830 – Tarbat Ness on the east coast of mainland Scotland was automated in 1985

1830 – Mull of Galloway on the south-west corner of mainland Scotland was automated in 1988

1831 – Dunnet Head on the north coast of mainland Scotland was automated in 1989

1833 – Girdle Ness on the east coast of Scotland near Aberdeen was automated in 1991

1833 – Barra Head south of the Outer Hebridean island of Barra was automated in 1980

1833 – Lismore on the Inner Hebridean island of Lismore was automated in 1965

1843 – Little Ross on Little Ross Island at the mouth of Kirkcudbright Bay was automated in 1960

1844 – Skerryvore off the southern end of the Inner Hebridean Island of Tiree was automated in 1994

1846 – Covesea Skerries on the south side of the Moray Firth was automated in 1984

1846 – Chanonry on the south side of the Moray Firth was automated in 1984

1846 – Cromarty on the north side of the Moray Firth was automated in 1985

1847 – Loch Ryan on the north side of Loch Ryan in south-west Scotland was automated in 1964

1849 – Noss Head near Wick on the north-east coast of the mainland was automated in 1987

1849 – Ardnamurchan on the west coast of Scotland was automated in 1988

1850 – Sanda on the southern tip of the Kintyre peninsula was automated in 1991

1851 – Hoy Sound High on the island of Graemsay in the Orkney Islands was automated in 1978

1851 – Hoy Sound Low on the island of Graemsay in the Orkney Islands was automated in 1966

1852 – Stornoway on the Outer Hebridean Isle of Lewis in Stornoway Harbour was automated in 1963

1854 – Out Skerries off the east coast of the Shetland Islands was automated in 1972

1854 – Muckle Flugga on the north end of the island of Unst in the Shetland Islands was automated in 1995

1854 – Davaar on the east side of the Kintyre peninsula in south-west Scotland was automated in 1983

1854 – North Ronaldsay in the Orkney Islands was automated in 1998

1857 – Ushenish on the island of South Uist in the Outer Hebrides was automated in 1970

1857 – Rona in the Inner Hebrides was automated in 1975

1857 – Rubha nan Gall in the Sound of Mull was automated in 1960

1857 – Ornsay in the Inner Hebrides near Skye was automated in 1962

1857 – Kyleakin on the mainland facing the Isle of Skye was automated in 1960 and discontinued when the Skye Bridge was built

1858 – Cantick Head at the entrance to Scapa Flow in the Orkneys was automated in 1987

1858 – Bressay on the east side of the Shetland Islands was automated in 1989

1859 – Douglas Head on the east side of the Isle of Man (replacing the tower of 1832) was automated in 1986

1859 – Ruvaal on the north end of the Hebridean island of Islay was automated in 1983

1860 – Fladda in the Inner Hebrides was automated in 1956

1860 – Corran on Loch Linnhe near the west coast of the mainland was automated in 1970

1861 – McArthur's Head on the east side of the Inner Hebridean island of Islay was automated in 1969

1862 – St Abb's Head on the east side of mainland Scotland was automated in 1993

1862 – Holburn Head on the north coast of mainland Scotland was automated in 1988

1862 – Butt of Lewis on the north end of the Outer Hebridean Isle of Lewis was automated in 1998

1864 – Monach, east of the Outer Hebridean island of North Uist, was discontinued in 1942

1865 – Skervuile in the Sound of Jura near the Inner Hebridean island of Jura was discontinued in 1945

1867 – Auskerry on a small island south-east of Stronsay in the Orkney Islands was automated in 1961

1869 – Loch Indaal on the Inner Hebridean island of Islay was never manned

1870 – Scurdie Ness on the east coast of mainland Scotland was automated in 1987

1870 – Stoer Head on the north-west coast of mainland Scotland was automated in 1978

1872 – Dubh Artach, west of the Inner Hebridean island of Colonsay, was automated in 1971

1873 – Turnberry on the south-west coast of mainland Scotland was automated in 1986

1875 – Chicken Rock off the south end of the Isle of Man was automated in 1961

1877 – Holy Island Inner in the Inner Hebrides was automated in 1976

1880 – Langness on the south-east coast of the Isle of Man was automated in 1996

1885 – Fidra on the south side of the Firth of Forth was automated in 1970

1886 – Ailsa Craig off the south-west coast was automated in 1990

1887 – North Carr, the only manned lighthouse vessel, stationed off the east coast of mainland Scotland, was automated in 1975

1892 – Fair Isle South in the Shetland group was the last lighthouse to be automated in 1998

1892 – Fair Isle North in the Shetland group was automated in 1981

1893 – Helliar Holm on the Orkneys' main island was automated in 1967

1895 – Rattray Head off the east coast of mainland Scotland was automated in 1982

1895 – Sule Skerry, west of the Orkney Islands, was automated in 1982

1896 – Stroma in the Pentland Firth was automated in 1996

1897 – Tod Head on the east coast of mainland Scotland was automated in 1986

1898 – Noup Head on the Orkney island of Westray was automated in 1964

1899 – Flannan Isle, west of the Isle of Lewis in the Outer Hebrides, was automated in 1971

1900 – Tiumpan Head on the east coast of the Isle of Lewis in the Outer Hebrides was automated in 1985

1900 – Killantringan on the south-west coast of mainland Scotland was automated in 1988

1901 – Barns Ness on the east coast of mainland Scotland was automated in 1986

1902 – Bass Rock off the east coast of mainland Scotland was automated in 1988

1904 – Hyskeir in the Inner Hebrides was automated in 1997

1905 – Holy Isle Outer in the Inner Hebrides was automated in 1977
1909 – Neist Point on the north-west corner of the Inner Hebridean island of Skye was
automated in 1990
1912 – Rubh' Re located on the north-west coast of mainland Scotland was automated in 1986
1914 – Maughold Head on the west side of the Isle of Man was automated in 1992
1915 – Copinsay off the south-east corner of the main island of the Orkneys was
automated in 1991
1916 – Clythness off the east coast of mainland Scotland was automated in 1964
1924 – Duncansby Head on the north-east corner of mainland Scotland was automated in 1997
1929 – Eshaness on the north-west coast of
the main Shetland Island was
automated in 1974
1958 – Strathy Point on the north coast of
mainland Scotland was automated
in 1997
1968 – Calf of Man rebuilt on the
south-west tip of the Isle of Man was
automated in 1995

Strathy Point was the last manned light
built by the Northern Lighthouse Board.
Some lights have been built since but they
were run by computers from the beginning
and do not have the romantic character of
the manned lights. Examples of these are
Fife Ness built in 1975 on the east coast of
mainland Scotland, Fethaland built in 1977, Ve Skerries built in 1979 on the west coast of
mainland Shetland, and Haskeir, Gasker and Monach built in 1997 west of Lewis to help
guide the oil tankers.

Dunnet Head

Lighthouse automation has caused great controversy worldwide. First, there was
concern for the families whose profession for generations had been taking care of the lights.
In Scotland all of the keepers were made redundant by 31 March 1998. Many people still
feel that the loss of the lighthouse keeper is one step backwards instead of forwards. With
the advent of the computer the need for a human to man the lighthouses became
unnecessary, but the replacement of dedicated men and women with a machine seems
frightening when it involves saving lives.

A good example of what I mean occurred at our lighthouse, Eshaness, recently.
During a series of thunderstorms lightning struck a transformer near the station and the
electricity went out. The attendant keeper, Leslie Johnson, concerned by the severity of the
storms, went to the lighthouse to check. When he entered the tower he could smell hot
wires and, immediately inspecting everything, he found the electricity was off and the light
was running on batteries. Calling Edinburgh to ask why he had not been notified, the
response was that the watch had noticed something but since it looked like a common power

dip they did not notify the attendant. This was a logical conclusion to reach. The batteries would have clicked on immediately at the loss of power and the light would have come back on. What was not evident on the computer in Glasgow was the extensive damage done to the wiring. Thank goodness Leslie was concerned enough to inspect the tower and discover the scorched wires.

One of the major problems with automation, or in some cases the discontinuation of the operation of the lighthouse, has been what would happen to the buildings at each station. Many of the buildings were well-known landmarks with historic significance. In some areas the stations were abandoned and allowed to die a slow and ugly death. In other areas the Board is trying to reverse this trend and is making efforts to find buyers for the buildings.

The Northern Lighthouse Board has become a world leader in lighthouse preservation and has developed a system to dispose of lighthouse property – a successful paradigm that others have begun to follow. After automation was completed and the keepers removed, the towers were made into self-contained units separate from all other property. In some of the buildings where the tower was attached to the keepers' accommodation, doors were turned into walls. Once access to the tower was blocked, the keepers' accommodation was made available for purchase. The tower would remain in control of the Lighthouse Board until the light was discontinued. In some instances local government bodies became owners of the stations but the majority of the properties were sold on the open market.

This was accomplished through a bidding system that is standard in Scotland for purchasing property. After a period of advertising, a call for sealed bids was made and all interested purchasers would have their solicitors submit a bid. The Board would consider these, usually taking the highest bid, although they did not have to do so. After the property was sold the new owners were required to sign a covenant with the Northern Lighthouse Board to maintain the property to the standards of the Board. As an owner of one of the stations (excluding the tower) my husband and I must keep it painted and in good repair. The lighthouse keepers are gone and have been replaced by a group of homeowners who are not only taking care of their home but also preserving the lighthouse property for generations to come.

Two significant and remarkable things happened as a result of this system. Most important, the lighthouse stations did not become derelict or abandoned – with two exceptions. The owner of Noss Head lived far away and did not get back often to visit, and being so close to Wick it was easy for people to access the property. Over a period of a few years the assistant keeper's accommodation was destroyed. The property has now been sold to a local trust and hopefully someone watches over the property full-time and the vandalism is over. At the time of writing this book the keepers' accommodation at Duncansby Head in north-east mainland Scotland is in a badly run-down condition. The board has not been able to sell the property due to the high cost of removing asbestos from the building and the keepers' accommodation is being considered for demolition. The Northern Lighthouse Board's system has managed to keep the rest of the property surrounding the towers in a good state of repair.

The second benefit from the system has been the unique ways in which keepers' accommodation are being used. They have become museums, visitors centres, self-catering facilities and bed and breakfasts. One station has become a luxury hotel and another a retreat for Buddhist monks. Many have become private homes. As one of the owners whose use is a private home I am thankful for the foresight of the Northern Lighthouse Board. Many other countries are looking at the Scottish system to see if it will suit their lighthouse stations – let's hope it will help them preserve their historic buildings in the same way.

THE STEVENSON FAMILY

When talking about lighthouses in Scotland you constantly come across the name Stevenson. Most of us are familiar with Robert Louis Stevenson, the author of *Kidnapped, Treasure Island* and *The Strange Case of Dr Jekyll & Mr Hyde*. Some even know that he was from Scotland. What is not common knowledge is that he was trained as an engineer before he escaped into writing. Members of his family were the driving force behind and engineered the Northern Lighthouse Board's lighthouses built from 1799 through to early 1938.

The story of this fascinating family begins not with a Stevenson but with Thomas Smith. By the time he was 30 Smith was a successful businessman in Edinburgh where he owned an Arctic whaler and the Greenside Company, which manufactured whale-oil lamps in containers. Wanting to find a new market for his whale-oil lamps he turned to lighthouse illuminants. Whale oil had not been used for lighthouses in Europe, but in the United States sperm oil was used at Little Brewster Island off Boston Harbour. Smith favoured construction of lighthouses with lamps aided by reflectors instead of coal-fire beacons. He sold his first lighthouse lamp to Leith Pier Beacon.

After Aimé Argand of Switzerland invented a lamp burner, which had a tubular wick between metal tubes that let air to the inner surface of the flame and a glass chimney that funnelled the smoke away, it became possible to build more effective light sources for lighthouses. Smith began to use the Argand lamps and his proposal to use this technology at the Isle of May Light brought him to the attention of the newly formed Northern Lighthouse Board. He was asked to supervise the construction, lighting and maintenance of the Board's first four lights, Kinnaird Head, North Ronaldsay, Eilean Glas and the Mull of Kintyre. He was given the title of Engineer to the Northern Lighthouse Trust in 1786.

While constructing the lighthouses he married a widow, a Mrs Alan Stevenson, and thus he became associated with the Stevenson family. Mrs Alan Stevenson was the mother of Robert Stevenson, the first of the engineers with the Stevenson name, and Thomas Smith influenced Robert greatly by sharing his enthusiasm for lighthouses and books. At the age of

15, Robert accompanied his stepfather to work on Kinnaird Head Lighthouse in 1787 and later that summer to the Mull of Kintyre Lighthouse. These trips began his interest in lighthouses. After much persuasion, Thomas Smith was able to convince his wife that Robert would be happier as an engineer than a minister, which was the profession she had chosen for him. Robert was sent to the Anderson Institute, one of the first technical schools in Britain.

For five years Robert Stevenson worked under Thomas Smith as an apprentice engineer for the Lighthouse Board while he attended classes at the University of Edinburgh. When he was 26 Robert became a fully-fledged lighthouse engineer. From this point forward he did most of the lighthouse work while Thomas Smith spent his time running the business.

The final link between Smith and the Stevensons was forged when Robert married Jean, Thomas Smith's second daughter by his first wife, and the rest of the Stevenson engineers were descended from this marriage.

Robert was obsessed with the vision of building a lighthouse on Bell Rock in the North Sea off Dundee, and for six years he refined the idea. In December 1799 a huge storm hit the east coast of Scotland and 70 ships were lost including a British warship, The York. After the disasters caused by the storm, Robert was able to convince the Northern Lighthouse Board to ask the British Government for funds to build a lighthouse on Bell Rock. From 1800 onwards he bombarded the Board with requests for a chance to build the lighthouse – even though his appeals were eloquent, the Board was indifferent. The main objections were that Robert had built only one lighthouse on his own and the projected cost of £41,685.

In 1805 the Commissioners sought the services of John Rennie to build the lighthouse on Bell Rock, and after evaluating it, Rennie concluded that it would be practical. Influenced by a second positive opinion, the Northern Lighthouse Board drew up a bill for the House of Commons for construction of the lighthouse. The first bill failed, but the second was passed in July 1806, and John Rennie was made Head Engineer with Robert Stevenson assisting. Rennie, a popular engineer, was away most of the time trying to keep all of his other projects going, so Robert found himself actually in charge. It took three years for Robert to convince the Board that they should make him the Head Engineer for Bell Rock. Actual work on the lighthouse began in August 1807 and the light was finally established on 1 February 1811.

Many hail the construction of Bell Rock as one of the greatest feats in lighthouse engineering ever accomplished and newspapers of the time called Bell Rock "one of the wonders of the modern world". It certainly made Robert Stevenson the most famous lighthouse builder of his time. Robert continued to build lighthouses for the Northern Lighthouse Board and others. The list of Scottish lighthouses designed by Robert Stevenson includes Inchkeith, Start Point, Bell Rock, Corsewall Point, Point of Ayre, original Calf of Man, Sumburgh Head, Rinns of Islay, Buchan Ness, Cape Wrath, Tarbat Ness, Mull of Galloway, Dunnet Head, Girdle Ness, Barra Head and Lismore.

Robert's oldest son, Alan, was extremely bright but his health was not good. It was evident as early as Secondary School that he did not have the strength needed to be a lighthouse engineer. He was a solitary type who disliked crowds and was happier reading poetry and the classics than doing anything else. This was totally unacceptable to his father and Robert pressured his son into engineering. Alan bent to his father's will. By 1835 Alan had been an apprentice to the Northern Lighthouse Board for seven years, Clerk of Works for five years, and an equal partner in his father's business. He had during that time designed seven lighthouses under his father's supervision. He had been involved with studying the Fresnel lens and completing a review of lenses in Scottish lights.

Bass Rock

His first big chance came when the Commissioners gave him the responsibility of being builder and engineer for Skerryvore. Skerryvore is a group of rocks 10 miles south of the Inner Hebridean island of Tiree where most of the rocks are permanently submerged underwater. Alan began construction of the lighthouse on 5 May 1838. The building of Skerryvore was difficult with weather delays and long cold nights on the ship waiting to get onto the rock. It became evident the construction could not be completed without a barrack on the island. Right after the barrack was erected the next winter storms destroyed it. In 1839 they built a stronger barrack so work could progress. It took 217 days for 20 men to cut the hole to hold the foundation of the tower. The hole was completed in 1840. After that the building went fairly smoothly and was completed in July 1842. It took another season to finish the details, including an original optic apparatus that incorporated a Fresnel lens. On 1 February 1844 the light was turned on.

The years at Skerryvore weakened Alan's health even further and he returned to Edinburgh a sick man. Robert Stevenson resigned on 16 November 1843 at the age of 70. Alan applied for the position as chief engineer on the same day his father resigned and he was appointed immediately. However, the Board expected him to keep his position as chief of works as well as building ten new lights from 1844 to 1854. Those lights included Skerryvore, Covesea Skerries, Chanory, Cromarty, Loch Ryan, Noss Head, Ardnamurchan, Sanda, and Hoy High and Low. Alan's health began to deteriorate drastically and he resigned on 9 February 1853. He died in 1865, spending his last days translating the Ten Hymns of Synesius from Greek. In the introduction to his translations he said: "It pleased God in 1852 to disable me, by severe nervous affliction, for my duties as Engineer to the Board of Northern Lighthouses; and I took to beguiling my great suffering by trying to versify the whole Ten Hymns of Synesius. During many an hour, the employment helped to soothe my pains."

Alan's brother, David Stevenson, became chief engineer for the Northern Lighthouse Board in 1853 after Alan resigned. Prior to that, his biggest project for the Board had been the supervision of the building of a road to the Mull of Kintyre Lighthouse. David was a thorough and dedicated worker who was disciplined and devoted to procedures and systems. He was more of a manager than a pioneer like the Stevensons before him. Due to the heavy management load and some two years of illness, David suggested the Commissioners consider his brother, Thomas, be appointed with him as joint general engineer to the Board. Two departments would be developed. One, overseen by the Stevensons, would design and plan new lighthouses and make recommendations on changes to fuel sources and lenses. The other would manage the day-to-day business of inspection tours, preparing accounts, buying stores and managing keepers. The Board agreed and appointed a manager to handle the daily operations.

The Crimean War started the same year as his appointment and one of Britain's major goals was to dispatch a fleet to blockade the White Sea ports of Archangel and Murmansk. This meant the fleet would have to go around the north of Scotland, Norway and Lapland to reach Russian waters. As a result of the need for a northern passage, David's greatest building challenge came with Muckle Flugga off the northernmost island of the Shetland group, Unst, a location farther north than St Petersburg or the southern tip of Greenland.

Sanda

The lighthouse was to be built on a rock known as "Great Precipice". Construction was started on a temporary light on the "Flugga" in July 1846 and the light was established on 11 October that year. David was convinced that only a permanent light would stand up to the storms and gigantic waves around Unst. After much fighting between the Northern Lighthouse Board and Board of Trade, the go-ahead for a permanent lighthouse on Muckle Flugga was given in June 1855. For the first time in the history of marine engineering a 64-foot brick tower was built on foundations sunk 10 feet into the rock at the northern limit of the British Isles. In 1856 over 100 people worked on the rock from April to November. Bricks had been chosen for the tower because they could be shipped in small boats and thrown ashore. The entire project cost £32,000 and the light was completed and went into service in January 1858. His brother, Thomas, joined David in the design of the station. Many consider David's building of Muckle Flugga as great an accomplishment as his brother's building of Skerryvore or his father's building of Bell Rock. Many storms in which waves washed over the top of the tower have battered the lighthouse, and flying rocks and gigantic swells have damaged walls and doors. However, it is said that from its establishment to current times Muckle Flugga never let in one drop of water.

Under the new system David and Thomas Stevenson were to build 29 lights from 1854 to 1878. Lights constructed by the team were Out Skerries, Muckle Flugga, Davaar, new light at North Ronaldsay, Ushenish, Rona, Rubha nan Gall, Ornsay, Kyleakin, Cantick Head, Bressay, Douglas Head, Ruvaal, Fladda, Corran, McArthur's Head, St Abb's Head, Holburn Head, Butt of Lewis, Monach, Skervuile, Auskerry, Loch Indaal, Scurdie Ness, Stoer Head, Dubh Artach, Turnberry, Chicken Rock, Holy Island Inner and Langness. In 1881 David retired and Thomas remained alone as the Northern Lighthouse Board's senior engineer.

Thomas Stevenson's main interest was in lighthouse optics. His first big contribution to the field was the "apparent light", a new method of lighting pier heads and sunken rocks. The concept was simple. Prisms were placed in the beacon and then a light beam was projected from a nearby shore that would produce a light that appeared to be coming from the beacon itself. The idea worked so well it was used for the next fifty years. Later he also invented a new "condensing" device, which allowed the light to show in different directions in varying strength according to the distance needed. On 1 December 1886 the multidirectional light was used for the first time in the new light on the Isle of May. When Thomas designed new leading lights at Button Ness for the Trinity House of Dundee he introduced another concept in lighting. The new light source contained a dioptric holophotal light that was an adaptation of the Fresnel lens, but instead of using mirrors with fans above the lens to pass on the light it enclosed the light in a prismatic glass casing. This was considered Thomas's greatest contribution to lighthouse engineering.

Waves were another major interest of Thomas Stevenson. He began his experiments with waves when he was assisting in the building of Skerryvore. His son once wrote in Records of a Family of Engineers: "He would pass hours on the beach, brooding over the waves, counting them, noting their least deflection." In two years Thomas made 267 experiments with waves that he published in the Journal of the Royal Society of Edinburgh. He concluded that Atlantic swells were always heavier than the ones from the North Sea.

Thomas Stevenson did not build spectacular lighthouses alone – he is known for his involvement with the construction of Dubh Artach, another difficult rock light, but it was carried out in conjunction with David. Thomas Stevenson's genius was directly involved with most of the Scottish lights through his innovations in the field of optics and his understanding of the environment in which the lighthouses were built. He died in 1887.

Thomas was the father of the famous author, Robert Louis Stevenson, and tried to force his son into engineering. It led to many fights and much resentment between the two. Even though eventually Robert Louis turned his back on engineering, he was interested in illumination, a legacy from his father. At the age of 20 he wrote a paper stating that gas was not a good option for lighthouses, which won him a silver medal. He also submitted a proposal to the Lighthouse Board for an "intermittent" light that was never acknowledged. Although he never practised as an engineer he wrote that he was proud of his family of lighthouse engineers. In 1880 he wrote: "Whenever I smell salt water, I know that I am not far from one of the works of my ancestors. The Bell Rock stands monument for my grandfather, the Skerry Vore for my Uncle Alan and when the lights come out at sundown along the shores of Scotland, I am proud to think they burn brightly for the genius of my father."

This brings us to the last of the Stevenson family whose name was significant as a Northern Lighthouse Board engineer. David Allen Stevenson was a son of David Stevenson and became known as David A. or Das. A man of detail and thoroughness, he was responsible for the designing of Fair Isle, Helliar Holm, Rattray Head, Sule Skerry, Stroma, Tod Head, Noup Head, Flannan Isle, Tiumpan Head, Barns Ness, Hyskeir, Holy Isle Outer, Neist Point, Rubh' Re, Maughold Head, Copinsay, Clythness, Duncansby Head and Eshaness.

With the death of David A. Stevenson in 1971 the period of a family devoted to building lighthouses came to an end. Between 1799 and 1938 they had built 97 lighthouses in Scotland and the Isle of Man. As a summary, and a reminder that the Northern Lighthouse Board continued to build lighthouses, here is the list of their senior engineers who built the lights of Scotland. (The title was changed to Engineer-in-Chief after 1972 and then changed to Director of Engineering in 1995.)

1786	*Thomas Smith*
1799	*Robert Stevenson*
1843	*Alan Stevenson*
1853	*David Stevenson*
1854	*David Stevenson and Thomas Stevenson*
1878	*Thomas Stevenson*
1885	*Thomas Stevenson and David A. Stevenson*
1886	*David A. Stevenson*
1938	*John Oswald*
1946	*J.D. Gardner*
1955	*Peter H. Hyslop*
1978	*John Williamson*
1987	*William Paterson*
2000	*Moray Waddell*

THE TOUR

Before we start our tour of the 31 Scottish lighthouses I have chosen for this book I want to share some words from someone else who spent six weeks visiting Scottish lighthouses. Sir Walter Scott is one of Scotland's most famous literary figures. He was a novelist, poet, historian and biographer, often considered both the inventor and the greatest practitioner of the historical novel. Scott was a prolific novelist, whose writing combined ordinary people and historical events, thus mixing cultures and classes. He was also a poet of national and international reputation writing, for example, *Lady of the Lake*.

Scott began his career as a lawyer. His appointment as sheriff-depute of the county of Selkirk in 1799 (a position he was to keep all his life) was a welcome supplement to his income, as was his appointment in 1806 as clerk to the Court of Session in Edinburgh. Taking advantage of his recess from court, in 1814 he sailed with Robert Stevenson around Scotland, as a guest of the Commissioners of the Northern Lights on their inspection cruise, in The Pharos. In five notebooks he recorded the details of his trip. The complete text was not published until 1838 and is now available from the Scottish Library Association entitled *The Voyage of the Pharos – Walter Scott's Cruise Around Scotland in 1814*. One of the tasks performed on that trip was to inspect Cape Wrath for a potential lighthouse. Sir Walter Scott writes:

Cape Wrath is a striking point, both from the dignity of its own appearance, and from the mental association of its being the extreme cape of Scotland with reference to the north-west. There is no land in the direct line between this point and America. I saw a pair of large eagles, and if I had had the rifle-gun might have had a shot, for the birds, when I first saw them, were perched on a

Flannan Isle

rock within about sixty or seventy yards. They are, I suppose, little disturbed here, for they showed no great alarm. After the Commissioners and Mr Stevenson had examined the headland, with reference to the site of a lighthouse, we strolled to our boat, and set sail for Lewis with light winds and a great swell of tide…The country behind Cape Wrath swells in high sweeping elevations but without any picturesque or dignified mountainous scenery. But on sailing westward a few miles, particularly after doubling a headland called The Stour of Assint, the coast assumes the true Highland character, being skirted with a succession of picturesque mountains of every variety of height and outline. These are the hills of Ross-shire – a waste and thinly peopled district….

Thus with Sir Walter Scott's words to lead us we are ready to explore some of the Scottish lights. In each lighthouse I have tried to write a little about the history and the uniqueness of each station along with information about the area in which the lighthouse stands.

I have chosen to start our tour on the south-west mainland of Scotland and from there we travel to the Hebridean Islands. Once we investigate some island lighthouses we explore examples of lighthouses on the west and north coast of mainland Scotland before we head for the Northern Isles of Orkney and Shetland. Our final region is the east coast of Scotland. It is an exciting exploration because each of the areas and lights are so different. I hope you enjoy it.

Turnberry

SOUTHERN SCOTLAND

TURNBERRY

One lighthouse is well known because it is the symbol for one of the world's most famous golf courses. People from all over the world have seen Turnberry Lighthouse on television when they watch the British Open – Turnberry hosted the 1977, '86 and '94 British Open Championships and the 1996 Amateur Championship. Since the resort chose the lighthouse as its emblem it is difficult to separate the lighthouse from the golf course; now the lighthouse and its walled garden stand proudly by the 17th hole. Turnberry is located on the west coast of Scotland less than an hour's drive from Glasgow Airport or 30 minutes from Prestwick Airport. (Nautical location is 55° 19′N, 4° 50′W.)

Turnberry was the first purpose-built golf resort constructed by the Glasgow and South Western Railway. It included a first-class hotel and rail links south to Girvan and north to Ayr and Glasgow. The club was founded in 1902 and by 1907 Turnberry was a recognised golfing centre. Its two courses are named Ailsa and Arran, after the islands of Ailsa Craig (11 miles offshore) and Arran, which can be seen while playing. Today the Ailsa course is regularly ranked among the top 20 courses in the world while the Arran is rated by some to be an even more difficult challenge. There is a Turnberry saying that if you can't see Ailsa Craig, it's raining, and if you can see it, then it's about to rain.

The lighthouse preceded the golf course. It was built in 1873 and the engineers were David and Thomas Stevenson. The keeper's accommodation is a two-storey building with an

80-foot-high tower. The beacon flashes white every 15 seconds with a range of 22 miles. Turnberry was always a popular posting for keepers as they received honorary membership of the golf club during the time they worked at the lighthouse.

Near the lighthouse at the golf course's 9th hole is the 14th-century Turnberry Castle, significant in Scottish history as Robert the Bruce was born there (in the older castle) on 11 July 1274. He was the first of a large family born to Robert Bruce, 6th Lord of Annandale, and Marjorie, Countess of Carrick. Turnberry Castle was home to the earldom of Carrick. A pact called the Turnberry Bond between the Bruce families was made at this castle, which drastically affected what happened to make Robert the Bruce King of Scotland. It is also where the fight for the independence of Scotland began when Robert the Bruce attacked Turnberry Castle, in the bay at Maidens.

Turnberry Lighthouse was automated in 1986 and sold to a private buyer. Eventually the golf resort purchased the lighthouse, but despite spending millions on renovating their facilities the lighthouse shows signs of neglect. On my last visit the outside of the property was newly painted and the lower windows boarded up. From a distance it looked like the building was well cared for, but on closer inspection the upper windows were open to the elements. I could see where rubble had fallen from the upper windows to the ground around the lighthouse, which made me wonder about the state of the inside of the building. I am hoping that the next time I visit, the inside of the building will be renovated. There is some hope, as the US firm Starwood Lodging Corporation, a hotel management and operating company, acquired the 132-room Turnberry Hotel and the 800-acre golf resort, including the lighthouse for a total purchase price of £35.5 million (US $51.5 million) in 1997, and there is discussion of turning the lighthouse into luxury apartments.

CORSEWALL POINT

Just down the road from the former small fishing village of Kirkcolm, with its attractive terraces of white single- and two-storey cottages, can be found Corsewall Point Lighthouse.

Corsewall Point

Corsewall Point

This lighthouse guards the northern tip of the Galloway peninsula where Loch Ryan and the North Channel between Ireland and Scotland meet. (Position on the Nautical Chart is 55° 00.5′N, 5° 09.5′W.) The Kintyre Peninsula, Arran, the Firth of Clyde, Ailsa Craig and even the coast of Ireland can be seen from the lighthouse. The waters that it watches over are busy with up to twenty ferries daily sailing between Stranraer and Cairnryan to Larne in Ireland and Douglas in the Isle of Man.

Corsewall Point Lighthouse was established in 1816 to "mark the Scottish side of the channel between the Rinns of Galloway and Ireland". Robert Stevenson was the engineer and Lachlan Kennedy, a former clerk during the building of Bell Rock, was in charge of the works. The design included a round tower 112 feet high with the keepers' houses detached from the tower so that smoke from domestic fires would not damage the apparatus. This is one of the few towers to which Robert Stevenson added some ornamentation in the form of protective battlements, which can be seen near the tower's base. The tower has a range of 18 miles and its light flashes 5 whites every 30 seconds. The sturdiness of the facility was tested during World War Two when it was slightly damaged during the great bombing raids on the city of Belfast.

Mull of Galloway

The lighthouse is a popular tourist attraction and is situated on one of Britain's most popular birdwatching trails. Nearby is the Iron Age fort of Dunskirkloch. The Scottish Natural Heritage designated the shoreline around the station as a Site of Special Scientific Interest because it contains some of the oldest exposed rocks in Europe. In nearby Kirkcolm can be found the Kilmorie Cross, which was carved during the 10th century and whose design combines Christian and pagan Scandinavian images, unique in the south-west part of Scotland.

Mull of Galloway

It came as no surprise when the light was automated in 1994, the keepers removed and their accommodation sold. My husband and I made a bid on the property with the idea of turning it into a self-catering facility but it was not to be. The keepers' facilities, watchroom, and the 20-acre grounds have now been turned into a luxury hotel that says in its brochure: "Corsewall Lighthouse Hotel invests the charm and romance of an 1825 functioning lighthouse with the comforts of a small unique luxury hotel and restaurant." There is much debate among lighthouse aficionados whether the changes to the lighthouse have been good ones. Many believe that it has lost its character even though the beacon is still turned on every night. No matter what your attitude is about its current use, it is a beautiful place and a magnificent lighthouse.

To reach the lighthouse you must watch the signs carefully. Take the A718 from Stranraer to Kirkcolm and about a mile beyond the village, where the main road joins the B738, turn right. At the next minor junction turn left and at the following junction turn right continuing down the hill. Just past Barnhill Farms you will see the lighthouse.

MULL OF GALLOWAY

Most people think of the Mull of Galloway as only a lighthouse. In truth the lighthouse actually takes its name from the area where it is located. The region of the Mull of Galloway is the south-westernmost tip of Scotland – its western coasts have high cliffs while inland a rolling landscape is bordered by raised beaches and sandy shores. A strip of flat land links the Mull to the Galloway Hills and two completely different types of bay enclose this narrow part. To the north is the anchorage of Loch Ryan, with the ports of Stranraer and Cairnryan, and a merchant and naval history stretching back to before the Vikings. To the south is Luce Bay, a wide and shallow bay used by birds and holidaymakers. The Royal Air Force bombing range in the centre of its mouth scares off some tourists. The peninsula juts into the Irish Sea like a claw hammer and provides outstanding seascapes. (Position on the Nautical Chart is 54° 38.1′N, 4° 51.4′W.)

To go to the lighthouse you must drive to the end of the peninsula and this trip reinforces the marvellous contrasts of the area. When you reach the southern end of the Mull, a winding road across a rocky neck of land surrounded with wave-beaten cliffs and a lot of sea leads you to the car park. On a clear day you can see Cumbria, Ireland and the Isle of Man from the lighthouse that stands on a 210-foot-high headland. Established in 1828, the station cost £9,000 to build – the engineer was Robert Stevenson, who designed a station that included a graceful round wall surrounding an 81-foot tower. The accommodation is not connected to the tower. The entire complex is bordered by a low stone wall because experience had shown that high walls built for shelter caused "strong whirls of wind" in the courtyards of some lighthouses and interfered with the lighthouse keeper's lookout.

The beacon was originally an intermittent or occulting light, which meant two opaque shades were moved up or down to meet and obscure the light at fixed intervals. The periods of darkness were longer than those of light. In 1971 the lens was changed to a sealed beam in the Northern Lighthouse Electrification Programme. This increased its candlepower to 1,740,000. At the present time the beacon flashes white every 20 seconds with a range of 28 miles.

An RSPB bird reserve can be found within the wall near the lighthouse. You will find cliff-nesting seabirds such as countless cormorants, gannets, kittiwakes, guillemots, shags and razorbills wheeling through the air during the breeding season. Puffins have begun to appear on the cliffs, although they can be hard to spot as they ride the swell or tuck themselves into their burrows on the cliff face. A visitors centre is open in summer with rangers to

advise visitors. Next to the lighthouse, a path, definitely not for the faint-hearted, twists down the cliff to the sea. A much safer-looking descent goes round the southern cliffs and a number of caves before climbing back to reach a set of ancient earthworks that probably marked the entrance to a large Iron Age fort.

The station was automated in 1988 and the keepers removed. The Northern Lighthouse Board did not sell the property but maintained the accommodation as holiday homes for their employees. Recently they have turned one of the keeper's houses into a self-catering facility open to the general public.

MULL OF KINTYRE

Far have I travelled, and much have I seen
Darkest of mountains with valleys of green
Vast painted deserts, the sun sets on fire
As we carries home to, the Mull of Kintyre

Mull of Kintyre, oh mist rolling in from, the sea
My desire, is always to be here, oh Mull of Kintyre

Mull of Kintyre

Mull of Kintyre

These words from a song composed by Paul McCartney brought fame to a difficult-to-reach lighthouse found on the southern end of the Kintyre peninsula. (Position on the Nautical Chart is 55° 18.6′N, 5° 48.1′W.) Many call the entire peninsula the Mull but only the tip of this is truly the Mull – from the Norse word muli, or Gaelic maol, both of which mean headland. To get to the lighthouse from Glasgow take the A82 to Tarbet, then the A83 to Tarbert, which goes on to run the length of Kintyre to Campbeltown. After you reach Campbeltown you proceed south until you find the road that goes west to the lighthouse. This is the most frightening and difficult journey to a lighthouse I have ever travelled. It is not for everyone. Just getting to the car park where the access road to the lighthouse begins is terrifying. After you reach the car park at the high pass called the Gap, the road twists and turns 1,000 feet down the cliff to reach the lighthouse. In 1782 storm after storm hit the Scottish coast. Many lives were lost including those aboard two herring boats that were

rounding the Kintyre peninsula. As a result the Mull of Kintyre became the second lighthouse to be built after the Northern Lighthouse Board was formed in 1787. It was designed by Thomas Smith, the first Northern Lighthouse Board engineer and placed in operation in October 1788. Although the lighthouse is located on Scotland's mainland the actual construction in such a remote locality in 1788 was almost impossible. Delivering the building materials to the site by sea was impractical because of the hazardous nature of the shoreline on which it was built. Everything had to be brought across the barren moorland by packhorse from Campbeltown 12 miles away.

The station was rebuilt in the early 1800s to give it more permanence. In 1906 the beacon was altered from a fixed light to a group-flashing light and the power increased from 8,000 to 281,000 candlepower. In 1976 the candlepower was increased again to 1,575,000. Today the light's character is 2 whites every 20 seconds and the beacon has nominal range of 29 miles.

The first keeper at this lighthouse was Matthew Harvie, a local crofter, who was paid £50 per annum with the usual grazing and fuel perks. His appointment was appropriate as there was a long established tradition of the occupiers of "Harvie's Acres" at Bailemoil keeping a light burning in their kitchen window to warn seamen off the rocks.

Another Mull of Kintyre keeper whose name will go down in history is David Murchie. On 2 June 1994 a Chinook helicopter crashed on the south face of Beinn na Lice, on the peninsula just up the road from the lighthouse. Murchie was the first person on the scene and he described it as follows: "I heard a dull thud, followed by a whooshing...then silence. I knew immediately what had happened. I knew the helicopter had crashed." He rushed to the scene, frantically moving from body to body trying to revive the victims. But all twenty-nine passengers, which included the four crew, as well as nine army intelligence officers, six MI5 officers and ten members of the RUC Special Branch, were already dead. The Queen honoured David Murchie for his efforts.

SANDA

One of the most unique lighthouses in the Northern Lighthouse system is found on the island of Sanda. Sanda lies on the west side of the entrance to the Firth of Clyde and is approximately 7 miles east-south-east of the Mull of Kintyre, a short distance from Campbeltown. (Position on Nautical Chart 55° 40.4′N, 5° 34.9′W.) The island is a 60- to 90-minute boat trip from Campbeltown. Covering an area of about a square mile (314

Sanda

acres), it lies less than 2 miles offshore from the village of Southend, which makes it easily seen from the mainland. Its name suggests sand and indeed the Old Norse name for this island was Sandtange, meaning sandpit. The island does boast a large sandpit known as "Oitir Buidhe" in Gaelic, meaning yellow sandpit. The Danes knew the island as Havin, meaning anchorage. Just off the coast of Sanda you will find Sheep Island and Glunimore Island – as the name suggests, Sheep Island provides little more than grazing for sheep and Glunimore is too small for any commercial use. On the north side of Sanda there is an excellent anchorage for small vessels, formed by a shallow sandy bay protected by the nearby Sheep Island.

The lighthouse on the southern end of Sanda was established in 1850 and the engineer in charge of its construction was Alan Stevenson. As far back as 1825 requests had been made for the building of a light on the island. The island is a key shipping stop because it forms a turning point in the Clyde for ships passing through the North Channel between Scotland and Ireland. When the Christiania of Glasgow, outward bound in bad weather, was lost on the nearby Paterson's Rock, Trinity House proposed that the light at the Mull of Kintyre be moved to Sanda. The Northern Lighthouse Commissioners rejected this, although they were willing to place a beacon on Paterson's Rock. The continuing wrecks, however, caused the Northern Lighthouse Board to change its mind and to build a new lighthouse on the summit of the steep-sided Ship Rock.

Sanda

What makes this lighthouse so different is that the design incorporated a stone tower in three steps set against the face of the Rock. It is the only one of its kind in Scotland and this unique design was so costly to build it was a major contributing factor to the Northern Lighthouse Board overspending their budget in 1848. The lighthouse tower is 50 feet high and the beacon flashes white/red every 24 seconds. The white light reaches approximately 19 miles and the red 16 miles.

In 1871, 57 people lived on the island, making an uncertain living from fishing, kelp burning and farming. By the mid 1930s, the population was approximately 12, split between the lighthouse and one farm. Eventually the lighthouse keepers became Sanda's only permanent residents. Their families were withdrawn from the station in 1953, at which time Sanda became a "rock" lighthouse, relieved on a regular basis by an attending boat from Southend. The keepers spent four weeks on the island, followed by four weeks at their homes in Campbeltown and Oban. The lighthouse was relieved by boat from Southend until 1976 when the introduction of relief by helicopter improved the system. Sanda could now be reached in less than 10 minutes' flying time from Campbeltown, and the weather no longer became a major factor in getting to the lighthouse.

At first the boatmen lived on the island, and indeed in 1900 the RNLI silver medal and vellum was presented to the boatman, Daniel Dempsey, and his two sons for saving the crew of a schooner wrecked in heavy seas near the lighthouse. The rescue was carried out at great risk to themselves, using their own small boat.

There have been over thirty vessels wrecked near Sanda over the years. The 7,000-ton American "Liberty" ship, Byron Darnton, went ashore just 150 yards from the lighthouse in March 1946 and all 54 people on board, plus one Husky dog, were taken off by the Campbeltown lifeboat in an extremely hazardous rescue operation. The vessel later broke up, becoming a total loss. Local author Angus McVicar, in his book Rescue Call published in 1967, told the complete story of the disaster.

San

Rinns of Islay

There was an unusual occurrence in 1895 when the Northern Lighthouse Board's boat ran onto the Mull of Kintyre in dense fog going from McArthur's Head to Sanda. All aboard including one of the Northern Lighthouse Board's Commissioners were saved but the boat sank. An inquiry was held to determine the cause of the accident and it was decided that the foghorn was at fault. At that time it was blowing at four-minute intervals, not frequent enough for the conditions.

The lighthouse was automated in 1991 and is currently a private home. In 1979 an owner living in Southern England acquired the island – he put the island up for auction, but the bidding failed to reach the reserve price and it was withdrawn from the market. Even though the lighthouse and island are private, if you drive to the southern end of the Kintyre Peninsula you can see the lighthouse from the shore. It is also possible to get a boat to take you around the island.

HEBRIDES

RINNS OF ISLAY

The Isle of Orsay, owned by the Northern Lighthouse Board, is the home of the Rinns of Islay Lighthouse Station. The lighthouse sits across an inlet from the beautiful fishing village of Portnahaven with its pastel houses. (Position on the Nautical Chart is 55° 40.4′N, 6° 30.8′W.) The area is also known for its striking expanse of Lewisian gneiss, the oldest rock in Europe and half the age of the earth. To reach the Rinns of Islay Lighthouse you must take the ferry to Port Ellen on Islay, take the A846 to Bridgend and then travel the A847 down the long finger of the Rinns Peninsula to where the road ends in Portnahaven. The view of the lighthouse is magnificent from the village and well worth the drive.

Once in Portnahaven find a local fisherman to take you across the inlet to Orsay if you wish to inspect the lighthouse closely. Access is a short ten-minute ride in a small boat, but can be a problem. During the storms of 1877 and 1878 the lighthouse-attending boat from Portnahaven was wrecked trying to bring supplies to the keepers across this short distance.

Robert Stevenson designed the station that was built in 1825. The lighthouse construction cost £9,000, considered outrageous for the time – the cost was high because of the remote location. Stevenson also added innovations to the Rinns. Still visible today are porches on the balconies to give keepers protection when leaving the lantern room in stormy weather. The 95-foot white tower dominates the treeless island. The light has a range of 24 miles and flashes white every 5 seconds. In the 1870s William Thomson, later Lord Kelvin, described the Rinns of Islay, along with Buchan Ness and Little Ross, as "undoubtedly the three best revolving lights in the world".

The Rinns of Islay Lighthouse is one of the stations that employs the sealed beam

system of light production using lightweight sealed beam bulbs similar in size and shape to

car headlights made in the USA. These lights do not deteriorate or tarnish, being sealed behind an outer covering which creates a vacuum. The bulbs are mounted on a gearless revolving pedestal using a low-voltage rotary mechanism which is suited to a wide range of power supplies. Concave parabolic mirrors behind the bulbs focus the light. The main advantage of this system was that it was almost fully automatic from the time of installation. A light-keeper visited the lantern hourly until around 10 p.m. Then he did not have to go near it until extinguishing time the next morning unless summoned by the alarm bell. The sealed beam system was placed in the Rinns of Islay light in 1978 and increased the beacon's candlepower to 600,000.

Like all of the Northern Lighthouse Board's lights, the Rinns of Islay keepers were removed in 1998 and the station was completely automated. It still belongs to the Northern Lighthouse Board and there is no plan to sell the keepers' accommodation at the time of writing.

Skerryvore

SKERRYVORE

Skerryvore Lighthouse is one of the famous "rock" lights in the Northern Lighthouse Board system. The need for a lighthouse on Skerryvore was identified in a July 1814 Act of Parliament commonly known as the "May Act". The Skerryvore Lighthouse was built on a group of rocks 10 miles south of the Inner Hebridean island of Tiree, off the west coast of Scotland, and the highest rock is only 10 feet above Mean High Water Springs. Soon after the supervision of Scottish lights was taken over by Trinity House, some of the Elder Brethren appeared in Scotland for a voyage of inspection. They inspected the Skerryvore Rocks and the following is their report:

The day being very fine and calm, and the water smooth, steamed for the Skerryvore Rocks and at 2 p.m. saw the largest bearing NE about two miles, and 20 minutes past landed on it. A lighthouse no doubt can be built here without difficulty, as it is sufficiently large and high for the workmen to remain on the rock; a shed of things left there last remains on the rock. The Commissioners are making preparations for the erection on the largest Skerryvore and it is probable that ere long the Court will be called on for an opinion.

Sir Walter Scott landed on Skerryvore in 1814 on his tour. He stated:

...Hamilton, Duff and I resolved to land upon these rocks in company with Mr Stevenson. Pull through a very heavy swell with great difficulty and approach a tremendous surf dashing over black pointed rocks...I saw nothing remarkable in my way, except several seals...We took possession of the rock in the name of the Commissioners, and generously bestowed our own great names on its crags and creeks. The rock was carefully measured by Mr S. It will be a most desolate position for a lighthouse...the Bell Rock and Eddystone a joke to it...

From the beginning the Skerryvore project had problems. Alan Stevenson, only 30 years old, was appointed engineer for the project. He tried to survey the rock but only a preliminary triangulation was possible in 1834, and he was not able to finish the survey until the summer of 1835. The Board finally decided on stone for the tower and Tiree was fixed as the base of construction operations, though most of the supplies had to come from Oban 50 miles away. Quarries were established on Hynish and along with 14 others, James Scott, one of the stoneworkers for Bell Rock, was employed from 1836 to 1837.

Alan first attempted to follow the methods his father used on Bell Rock. Constant bad weather and difficulty with landing on the rock slowed construction. They had only 165 hours at work on the rock in the first season of 1838 but that allowed them to construct a barrack. This was destroyed by the sea during the winter, and the next year they built a stronger barrack in which living conditions were wretched for the workers. The cutting of the stone for the foundation of the tower took 20 men working for 217 days. In July 1842 the last stone of the parapet was laid, bringing the tower to 137 feet 11 inches. The tower contains 4,300 tons of masonry; hard gneiss from Hynish make up the first three courses and the rest is granite from the Ross of Mull. The walls are 2 feet thick at the top with the bottom being 9 feet 6 inches thick. The apparatus for the light was a Fresnel lens from Paris. In order to give a bright flash every minute the mechanism had eight lenses that revolved around a four-wick lamp. After much delay the light was finally established on 1 February 1844. (Position on the Nautical Chart is 56° 19.4′N, 7° 6.9′W.) Skerryvore had taken almost 6 years to build and cost £93,803. Robert Louis Stevenson hailed his uncle's Skerryvore light "as the noblest of all extant deep-sea lights".

The time and effort must have been worth it as the light is still functioning even after the original apparatus and rotation device were destroyed in a 1954 fire. The structure survived the fire and was repaired and placed back into operation. The current character of Skerryvore is flashing white every 10 seconds and the beacon has a range of 26 miles.

In 1984 the old Signal Tower was restored by the Hebridean Trust and turned into the Skerryvore Lighthouse Museum, which is located at Hynish on the Isle of Tiree. This small museum records the remarkable story of the design and construction of the lighthouse. Skerryvore was automated in 1994. The reconstruction and conversion of the Lighthouse Keepers' Cottages at Upper Square, purchased by the Trust in 1997, will provide homes for four island families at affordable rents.

HYSKEIR

Nine miles south-west of the Inner Hebridean island of Rhum is the tiny 10-acre island of Oigh-sgeir (maiden or virgin rock), known more commonly as Hyskeir. (Navigational location 56° 58′N, 6° 40.9′W.) The lighthouse by the same name guards the passage that links the Little Minch with the Sound of Mull. The island is aptly named as the base is made of hexagonal basalt columns rising to about 32 feet above sea level. Designed by David A. Stevenson, the 120-foot tower built in 1904 dominates the small island. The beacon flashes 3 white every 30 seconds and has a nominal range of 24 miles. Hyskeir is a "rock light" and as such the keepers' families lived on shore in Oban. Due to its remoteness it was one of two

Hyskeir

stations chosen by the Northern Lighthouse Board to test aircraft transporting supplies and keepers. A twin-engine four-seater aircraft was successfully tested in 1972.

For such a remote place the lighthouse station on Hyskeir has had its share of fame. Hyskeir Lighthouse was well known for its magnificent walled vegetable gardens. Each keeper had a garden that produced superb vegetables and the garden they kept jointly, known as the Rock Garden, became famous. It contained carrots, beetroot, cabbages, cauliflower, broccoli, onions and sprouts. Many in the lighthouse service who visited the station while the keepers were still there said it was the most productive lighthouse garden they had ever seen. The garden became so well known that a TV cookery show featured it and, following the keepers' appearance on television, the island also became well known for a one-hole golf course they had created.

As with most lighthouse stations the keepers who have served Hyskeir tell some interesting stories. The foghorn was located at the opposite end of the island from the main lighthouse building and an underground pipe connected the foghorn to the engine rooms. Compressed air was sent through the pipe to the foghorn to make the horn blow. One year it developed a leak. The keepers were given picks and shovels and told to trace and fix it. Not an easy job on an island made up of basalt column rock.

Another famous story from the keepers involved Maisie, an old nanny goat, who lived on the island. Before easy access by helicopter, offshore keepers kept a goat or two for fresh milk. Maisie was probably one of the last of the lighthouse goats. Keepers have reported that Maisie enjoyed delivering a hard bump to visitors' rear ends before she ran for cover and bleated with triumph. I wonder if Maisie was still around when the keepers built their golf course. If she was I bet she enjoyed that as much as they did.

Hyskeir was automated in 1997 and the keepers removed. The beacon is still operating and the station serves as a global climate prediction centre. Recent visitors say it is sad to see the once-productive walled gardens gone to seed and little evidence of the once well-known golf course.

The island can be reached by private fishing boat from Rhum which has a three-times-a-week Caledonian MacBrayne passenger ferry from Mallaig on the Scottish mainland. Hyskeir is a popular nesting site for terns and eiders, and has a large seal colony. In calm weather, it is also a good spot to see whales and basking sharks. In Gavin Maxwell's book Harpoon at a Venture, he wrote that the keepers had told him that basking sharks had been seen swimming under the bridge that links the two reefs.

NEIST POINT

Neist Point Lighthouse is located on the Duirinish peninsula to the south-west of Trotternish on the western tip of the Island of Skye. (Position on the Nautical Chart is 57° 25.4′N, 6° 47.2′W.) It has been guiding ships through the narrows of the Little Minch from its dramatic cliff-top position since 1909. Designed by David A. Stevenson, the tower stands 62 feet high but due to the station's 140-foot elevation above the sea, the light reaches out 24 miles. The light's character flashes white every 5 seconds.

Neist Point   When the Northern Lighthouse Board's automation programme began, Neist Point played an important role. In 1970 and 1971 Ushenish, Flannan Isle and Dubh Artach were

among the first lighthouses automated. Their gas-operated Dalén beacons were monitored by Neist Point 18 miles away. Neist Point's turn to be automated came in 1990. Currently it has a private owner and the three keepers' cottages are rented by the week as self-catering facilities – a secluded place for a holiday since most of the west coast of Duirinish has been uninhabited since the clearances of the 1830s.

The wreck of the Doris, a single-decked steel-screw steamer of 1,381 tons gross built by Wood Skinner and Co., Newcastle in 1900, lies down a slope on the south side of Neist Point. The Doris was 269 feet long, 40 feet wide and had a draught of 17 feet. The identity of the wreck, often incorrectly named "Doric" or "Derrick", was confirmed in 1984 when some divers from Edinburgh University discovered a brass nameplate giving the name of the ship and her builders.

The story of the wreck began on the morning of 12 July 1909 when the Doris, a Norwegian steamer, left Liverpool for Stettin carrying a general cargo. They had made good time until they hit a bank of thick fog just south of Skye. Fresh westerly winds and a strong tide made navigation difficult and the ship crashed onto the rocks. She was left stranded, her No. 1 hold rapidly filling with water. The crew, numbering thirteen, got off the ship safely including the captain, his wife, child and sister-in-law. The Doris spent the next two weeks perched precariously on the Neist Point rocks. During this time a considerable amount of her cargo was loaded onto two salvage coasters, the Fred and the Baron. By 23 July she had broken up in heavy seas. If you look carefully you can still see a few pieces of the wreck from the lighthouse.

To reach the lighthouse, once on the Isle of Skye head for Dunvegan. Drive south from Dunvegan on the A863, then turn onto the B884, following this road until there is a turn for Waterstein. Take this road and drive until the road ends at a car park. (The last time I did this I got lost, so watch carefully for the Waterstein sign.)

The car park is on the top of the cliffs, so from here you can either walk out over the cliffs to get views of Neist Point, the cliffs and the lighthouse, or you can go out through the gate at the end of the car park to the path leading down to the lighthouse. The walk takes about an hour – the steps are steep but have a handrail and are in good condition. The steep tarmac path takes you to the narrowest part of the headland from where you can get excellent views of the cliffs of Waterstein Head and the cliffs on Neist Point itself. The path then climbs again and finally descends to the lighthouse. From here you can wander round the rocks and watch the seabirds that nest on the cliffs of Neist Point – on a clear day you should be able to see Lewis and Harris. From the cliffs facing Neist Point there are excellent views back to the lighthouse, but take care on the cliff tops. On the 14 June 1999 an elderly woman fell from the footpath to the lighthouse and had to be rescued by helicopter.

ISLE OF ORNSAY

In February 1853 David Stevenson succeeded his brother Alan as Chief Engineer for the Northern Lighthouse Board. He recommended priority be given to building lighthouses at the north and south entrances of the sound between Skye and the mainland after the passing of Cardwell's Merchant Shipping Act of 1854. The Isle of Ornsay facility was established on

Isle of Ornsay   10 November 1857 along with Rubha nan Gall, Kyleakin, Rona and Ushenish. (Position on the Nautical Chart is 57° 8.6′W, 5° 46.4′W.)

David, joined by his brother Thomas Stevenson, engineered the facility. Thomas devised a new "condensing" apparatus by which the light shown varied in strength in different directions according to the distance from which it was required to be seen. This was important for lights like Ornsay that were set in narrow waters. The light has a nominal range of 12 miles and occults white every 8 seconds. The tower is 62 feet tall.

In 1895, at the Stevensons' recommendation, Ornsay became one of the first lights to be placed in the charge of just one keeper. This was the beginning of the removal of keepers from the lighthouse stations, a policy which automation continued. Ornsay was in the first group of lights to be automated, with the keeper withdrawn in 1962. This lighthouse is famous as Gavin Maxwell used the Sound of Sleat's lighthouses, including the Ornsay facility, while he researched his celebrated book on sea otters, Ring of Bright Water. Many of the scenes in the book are set around Ornsay Lighthouse. It is still possible to see otters there today if you sit quietly and watch.

To reach the lighthouse you must drive south after you cross the Skye Bridge to the Sleat peninsula between Loch Eishort and the Sound of Sleat. This area is known as "The Garden of Skye". You can drive to the village of Sleat or take a popular walk.

The walk is 12 miles long and should take about 4 hours on fairly good paths that lead to the lighthouse at the most southerly point of Skye. Go through the gate and follow the gently curving track across the moor. As the trail descends towards the sea, it narrows into a path. Here the scenery changes from featureless moorland into more of a garden-like area as trees and flowers border the path following the course of a small stream. The stream, which you will cross many times, descends into two waterfalls. The path narrows as it goes through a gate and passes the ruins of old crofts. Sheltered from the wind by trees, the ruined walls and the surrounding hills protect many plants like fuchsia and iris that add a lovely dash of colour to the scenery. Climb over a stile as the path continues on past a tiny harbour and cottage. After travelling through some boggy ground and climbing a hill, follow the direction of the peat cutting until you reach the top of the hill.

The easily seen path at the top of the hill will take you to some steps and your first glimpse of the lighthouse. Follow the path across the cliffs and out across a narrow path with the sea on either side. As the lighthouse is on a tidal island, access to the lighthouse is easy if timed correctly – when the tide is low, you can walk across to it. Be aware of the tides since at high tide the only access is by boat. There are steps leading up to the lighthouse from where you get excellent views out to Rhum and Eigg, and there are also the ruins of a chapel.

Butt of Lewis

BUTT OF LEWIS

The Butt of Lewis Lighthouse is located on the north-west corner of the Outer Hebridean Island of Lewis near the town of Ness. (Navigational location 58° 31′N, 6° 15.7′W.) This

spot is known as one of the windiest places in the United Kingdom.

David Stevenson designed the Butt of Lewis Lighthouse and in June 1859 the quotation of £4,900 submitted by John Barr & Co. of Ardrossan for "...dwelling house in brick and with lead roofs considered to be indispensable in view of the remoteness and exposure of the situation..." was accepted. There are extensive records of the building of this light which give insight into some of the difficulties involved with building lights that long ago. It was quite late in the year before Barr's could get their plant forwarded to the island, and the vessel containing part of the contractor's property was wrecked while attempting to land its cargo. This resulted in the masonry work being postponed until the spring of 1860. The Commissioners visited the Butt on 23 July 1860 and found "...work not so far advanced as had been anticipated". Later, on 24 March 1862, the Department of Trade was informed that "...the works at Butt of Lewis are so far advanced that the Commissioners expect it to be lighted in the autumn".

The tower stands 121 feet tall and there was quite a controversy over building the tower of brick. The original specifications for the bricks stated that they had to be "...similar to those used in the Edinburgh Gas Works chimney instead of common brick". When the Department of Trade asked for clarification, they received the following response:

Brick [normally] specified is the ordinary brick used for exposed places such as chimneys and is in all respects identical with what has been approved of in the whole of the lighthouse works which have been lately executed, including Corran, Pladda, McArthur's Head and St Abb's Head, all sanctioned last year and now in operation. Common brick in such a situation as the Butt of Lewis would be wholly inadmissible and would not stand the exposure to the sea...

Butt of Lewis

The tower has been standing tall for all of these years so their concern must have been erroneous.

Another problem during construction developed when the individual who had been engaged to build the tower's 168 concrete spiral steps went on strike demanding a penny a day increase in wages. Since he was the only person with the expertise to build the tower he got his rise.

A huge controversy developed between Stevenson and the Commissioners with the Department of Trade. The Commissioners favoured a flashing light but were overruled by the Trade Board, which insisted on "…a fixed light of the first order". The Commissioners subsequently notified Trinity House on 24 March 1859 that:

The Commissioners are of the opinion that the light should be a flashing white light of the first order, so as to distinguish it from Cape Wrath, which is alternate red and white, and from Stour Head, which the Commissioners mean to propose should be fixed…The adoption of a fixed light at such a station as Butt of Lewis could in the present day only be justified on some very special ground.

The Department of Trade prevailed and a fixed light was installed. On 8 March 1903 the staff at the Butt of Lewis were informed that the "character and measure of the power of the light" at the Butt would be changed in May of that year. While the work was in progress a temporary light (of the same character as the present light, although of lesser intensity) was put into operation: "The permanent light, when altered, will be flashing white, showing a flash every 20 seconds with a power of about 375,000 candles, and will be visible over the same bearings as the present light." Today the beacon flashes white every 5 seconds and has a nominal range of 25 miles.

Supplies were brought to the Butt of Lewis by boat into a small bay, known as Stoth, that is 400 yards from the lighthouse. This practice continued until 1960 when the roads on the Island of Lewis had improved enough to allow the supplies to come by ferry and then road to thelighthouse.

FLANNAN ISLE

Flannan Isle
The Flannan Isles are 21 miles west of the Isle of Lewis in the large area known as the Atlantic Outliers. (Position on the Nautical Chart is 58° 17.3′N, 5° 35.7′W.) Flannan's tiny

islands are sometimes called the Seven Hunters but in 1549 Dean Munro called them the Seven Haly Isles. He said they were inhabited only with "infinit wyld sheipe" that "cannot be eaten by honest men but make good tallow". The Bernera crofters still bring their sheep out to the islands to graze because of the high quality of the grass. The lighthouse is situated on the largest of the island group, 38-acre Eilean Mor (Big Island), which it shares with the ruins of the corbelled 6th-century St Flannan's Chapel. People living in Uig on Lewis still make an annual pilgrimage to worship at the ancient chapel.

The lighthouse was established and designed by David A. Stevenson in 1899. The lighthouse is set on a 200-foot cliff and because of its high elevation the white tower is only 75 feet tall. The beacon has a range of 20 miles and it flashes 2 white every 30 seconds. The facility was automated in 1971 and the keepers removed.

This lighthouse's claim to fame comes not from the removing of the keepers by automation, but the disappearance of three keepers in 1900. After being operational for little over a year, on 15 December a passing steamer noted in its log that the light was not working. Before receiving this information the lighthouse relief tender had sailed for the Flannan Isle Light. They sent back notice to Edinburgh on 26 December, declaring: "A dreadful accident has happened in the Flannans. The three keepers, Ducat, Marshall and the Occasional have disappeared from the island. On our arrival there this afternoon no sign of life was to be seen…Poor fellows must have been blown over the cliffs or drowned trying to secure or something like that."

The poet Wilfred Wilson Gibson wrote a poem entitled *Flannan Isle* and used a great deal of artistic licence in the poem. This set off many unconfirmed and often outrageous speculations about what had happened to the three men, including Sir Peter Maxwell Davies's chamber opera, The Lighthouse. One major myth that came from the poem was that the table was set for a meal. "We only saw a table spread, for dinner, meat and cheese and bread; But all untouched and no one there." This quote alone led to many stories, even though the official report says: "Kitchen utensils were all very clean, which is a sign that it must be after dinner some time they left."

The Northern Lighthouse Board official report from Superintendent Robert Muirhead places the responsibility for the disappearance on a rogue wave:

…I am of the opinion that the most likely explanation of the disappearance of the three men is that they have all gone down on the afternoon of Saturday 15 December to the proximity of the west landing, to secure the box with the moor-ing ropes etc., and that an expected large roller had come up on the island, and

a large body of water going up higher than where they were and coming down upon them had swept them away with resistless force…

Due to some lines in the ending of Gibson's poem – "Who kept the Flannan light, and how the rock had been the death of many a likely lad" – a lot of supernatural and ghost stories developed about the lighthouse station. It is important to point out that the station had only been open a year, since 7 December 1899, when the tragedy occurred. It is hard to imagine a new building being haunted by "the death of many a likely lad" in such a short time.

WEST COAST

ARDNAMURCHAN

The unspoiled Ardnamurchan peninsula lies due west of Fort William. Only 25 miles by 40 miles in size, its southern coast runs alongside Loch Sunart and the Sound of Mull, and its western edge is the most westerly point on the British mainland. A single-track road winds its way along the south side of the peninsula and panoramic views of the Hebridean islands of Muck, Eigg and Rhum are everywhere. The area abounds in otters, seals, porpoises and minke whales, and golden and sea eagles are frequently seen in the area along with red and roe deer, pine martens and wildcats.

      The Vikings landed here and stayed for over 500 years because a base on this peninsula was a highly important strategic lookout for Mull, Skye, the Argyll coast and even as far as the Western Isles. Poor land access also made it easy to defend. Place names such as Placaig, Acarsaig, Ormsaig and Grigadale are Norse in origin. The Vikings were not the first settlers on the peninsula; there is indication of ancient settlers going back 4,000 years.

Ardnamurchan

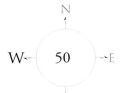

Scottish Lighthouses

Ardnamurchan

The peninsula lies on the edge of a unique geological feature known as the Ardnamurchan Ring Dyke Complex. This is the outer wall of a great volcano that erupted 55 million years ago, then collapsed forming the Achnaha plain and the surrounding hills. The area is dominated by the Ardnamurchan lighthouse that stands 118 feet above the rocks. (Position on the Nautical Chart is 56° 43.6′N, 6° 13.4′W.)

The lighthouse, designed by Alan Stevenson, was built in 1849 using pink granite from the island of Earraid in the Ross of Mull. The tower was not painted the traditional white of the Northern Lighthouse Board but left its original pink colour – its Egyptian style is alleged to be the only one of its kind in the world. The beacon flashing 2 whites every 20 seconds reaches 17 miles into the Little Minch. The station was automated in 1988. Originally purchased by a private buyer the local community felt the lighthouse was a national landmark and should be made available to everyone. They formed a trust, purchased the facility and turned it into a unique exhibition centre.

The centre is based in the principal keeper's house but also of interest is the engine room, the foghorn and the keepers' cottages. (A cup of tea can be obtained at the Stables Cafe.) The former head keeper's house is a fantastic place for anyone interested in lighthouses. Using video and computer technology, interactive displays for children, scientific experiments and exciting graphics, it gives a "hands-on" understanding of light, sound, communications and construction. You can see the original 550,000-candlepower lighthouse lens, listen to the keepers' radio conversations, learn how the lighthouse tower was built and even look at sound. The beautifully restored engine room and workshop demonstrates how the original foghorn operated and how the keepers maintained it. The foghorn and its platform are great places to watch whales and dolphins and in 1997 an all-weather viewing area was constructed allowing visitors to observe the activities in the sea regardless of wind and rain. The keepers' cottages have been fully restored and can be rented by the week. This unique centre is open daily from April to October and more information

Stoer Head

can be had from The Ardnamurchan Lighthouse Trust, Ardnamurchan Point, Kilchoan, Acharacle, Argyll PH36 4LN, Scotland; telephone: (01972) 510210; fax: (01972) 510396.

STOER HEAD

Out of David Stevenson's original list of forty-eight lighthouses needed to keep ships safe, the Northern Lighthouse Board chose eight, of which Stoer Head was one. An emphasis on economy by the Board of Trade kept this lighthouse from being built until 1870 – when Stoer Point was finally built David and Thomas Stevenson designed the station. It is located on the far west coast of Sutherland on the Rubha Stoer peninsula north of Lochinver and juts out into the Minch. (Position on the Nautical Chart is 58° 14.4′N, 5° 24′W.) Many consider the short 45-foot white tower to be squat in appearance, but the lighthouse

Stoer Head

sits on a cliff approximately 200 feet high so the light has enough elevation to reach 24 miles out into the Minch. The beacon flashes 4 white every 15 seconds.

The lighthouse is so remote that it was never a popular assignment for the keepers. After the station was automated in 1978 the Northern Lighthouse Board decided that the remote situation would make it a good place for holidays, and they have turned the two keepers' houses attached to the tower into holiday homes for their staff.

There are two major holiday attractions in the area. Beginning at the lighthouse car park there is a delightful walk along the cliff tops, with stunning views of the coastline and the Old Man of Stoer. There are several points where you get excellent views of the birds nesting or diving for fish in the sea below – the cliffs are dangerous so one must be careful along the edges.

The lighthouse is at the tip of the peninsula. About half a mile south of it is the area's most famous resident – a gigantic sea stack called the Old Man of Stoer. A great test for rock climbers is conquering the two hundred feet

N

S

of Torridonian sandstone that make up the stack. From the car park, climbers must proceed to the area of the stack where they follow an indistinct footpath ending at slippery rock platforms at sea level. To reach the stack climbers must cross a 30-foot channel by swimming across to the platform at the stack's base or use a ladder. Once on the stack it is a difficult climb that is sometimes made even harder by fulmar nests.

RUBH' RE

Rubh' Re Lighthouse is found on the Rudha Reigh peninsula in Western Ross. (Position on the Nautical Chart is 57° 51.4′N, 5° 48.6′W.) The different spelling of the lighthouse name from its location is confusing and frequently causes people to use the wrong spelling in relationship to the light. Looking at the Scots/Gaelic translation of the peninsula's name, we will find it means "the smooth/level/cleared point/headland". W.J. Watson in his seminal work on Ross-shire place names in 1904 gives "the smooth point" as his interpretation of Rudha. Rudha is the older spelling for Rubh from which the lighthouse takes its name.

The lighthouse sits on a point of land protruding into the Minch between mainland Scotland and the Isle of Lewis. Ships use Rubh' Re as a landmark to find Loch Ewe to its east and Loch Gairloch to its south. If you want to visit the station take the A832 to the village of Gairloch – the lighthouse is 12 miles from the village and 3 miles from the nearest dwelling. The lighthouse is currently operated as a bed and breakfast with many planned hikes and nature activities.

The lighthouse was designed by David Stevenson and built in 1912. In the early part of the century technology was often lacking in remote areas like Rubh' Re. In order to get a telephone service to the station a link was established between Strath on Loch Gairloch, Inverasdale on Loch Ewe and the lighthouse "for lifesaving purposes". It was also arranged to have a branch line to Melvaig for keepers to call in the Occasional when necessary. Kenneth

Rubh'Re

Rubh'Re

Macrae, the shopkeeper at Melvaig, was paid £4 per annum for taking these calls and passing them on to the Occasional.

The lighthouse's character is to flash 4 white every 12 seconds and the beam stretches 23 miles out into the Minch from a 25-foot tower which was automated in 1986. A World War Two incident makes one question the wisdom of lighthouses manned only by computers. In 1944 an American Liberty ship, the William H. Welch, missed the entrance to Loch Ewe and went ashore at Black Bay in a storm at night. Two Rubh' Re keepers set out to rescue the survivors across peat bogs in slush and snow. There is no doubt that many of the 14 survivors out of a crew of 74 owed their lives to these men. If a ship was wrecked at Black Bay today, a computer could definitely not go to the rescue.

According to one of the former Rubh' Re keepers, one of the station's funnier tales passed down from keeper to keeper involves a horse:

Many years ago nearly all lighthouses had a horse to collect stores. The story goes that the horse at Rubh' Re had become ill and this was reported to HQ. As the horse was getting old the keepers at the time decided to sell the horse and report its death to HQ. Unfortunately for them the superintendent decided about the same time to visit the station and was greeted from a nearby farm by a horse recognising the uniform.

What the superintendent did about this situation was not included in the story.

CAPE WRATH

Under the 1814 Act of Parliament commonly called "The Isle of May Act", the Northern Lighthouse Board among other things was given the authority to "erect and maintain such additional lighthouses upon such other parts of the coast and islands of Scotland as they shall deem necessary". As well as naming ten already erected, the preamble to the Act mentioned Galloway, Skerryvore, Cape Wrath, Shetland and Tarbat Ness as needing lights. Since 1802 shipping interests in London, Bristol and Liverpool demanded a lighthouse be built at Cape Wrath. One October night there had been three ships lost there and only two men saved.

If you go to the north-western tip of the Scottish mainland you will come upon Am Parbh (in Gaelic meaning "turning point") where the Pentland Firth meets the Minch. Paul Theroux called this area the "Empty Quarter" in his book *The Kingdom by the Sea*. Extending into the Atlantic Ocean the Cape Wrath headland is 368 feet high and is noted for its wildness and grandeur. The lighthouse stands 523 feet above the sea and faces the might of the Atlantic Ocean. The Isle of Lewis can be seen to the west, the Orkneys to the east, but to the north there is only the sea. (Position on the Nautical Chart is 58° 37.5′N, 5° W.) The lighthouse was engineered by Robert Stevenson and established in 1828 – the station cost £14,000 to build. The white tower is built of hand-dressed stone and the rest of the building is constructed of large blocks of granite quarried from nearby Clash Carnoch and stands 66 feet tall. The original light used reflectors to increase intensity – the current light has a character of flashing 4 white every 30 seconds and a nominal range of 24 miles.

Situated east of Cape Wrath are the Clo Mor Cliffs. These are the highest sheer cliffs in Great Britain, with a drop of 921 feet. They support an immense seabird colony with tens of thousands of puffins, razorbills, fulmars, kittiwakes and guillemots. Access is difficult and can be dangerous. There are two stacks situated one mile south of Cape Wrath whose names translate to the Old Woman and the Old Man. They are best reached by walking along the coast from the Cape. Diving is excellent in the area and there are many wrecks. Cape Wrath contains a "Site of Special Scientific Interest" (SSSI) and a "Special Protection Area" (SPA) for birds under the EU "Birds Directive".

The only problem with visiting Cape Wrath is that you must go through the Cape Wrath Bombardment Range. This issue came to media attention recently when a group of Scottish peace activists went to the control post of the Cape Wrath Range to protest against the US Navy using the range. London had offered the Pentagon the use of the range, and

Cape Wrath

two cruisers, *USS Anzio*, and *USS Cape St George*, and one destroyer, *USS Mahan*, were shelling Cape Wrath with their 5-inch guns. All of these vessels also carry Tomahawk Cruise missiles. The activists were worried stating: "The range area includes Clo Mor, the highest cliffs in Britain, and a seabird colony of international significance used by puffins, guillemots and many other species. Just offshore is Garvie Island, a tiny island where 1,000-pound bombs have been dropped regularly for decades." They should have added "Cape Wrath Lighthouse and its surrounding buildings" to their statement.

The station was automated in 1998 and the lighthouse tower and dwelling houses are listed buildings of architectural and historic interest. Slightly to the east and overlooking the lighthouse are the ruins of Lloyds' buildings – the famous insurance company constructed the buildings as a coastguard station.

Access is via the Cape Wrath Ferry and a minibus service located south of Durness – the minibus goes through the Cape Wrath Bombardment Range. The land between the Kyle of Durness and the lighthouse is known as the Parph and contains 11 miles of moorland.

NORTH COAST

DUNNET HEAD

Contrary to popular belief, John O'Groats is not the Scottish mainland's most northerly point. That honour goes to Dunnet Head, a few miles to the west. Dunnet Head is a sandstone promontory 341 feet high and the lighthouse on this headland was established in 1831. (Position on the Nautical Chart is 58° 40.3′N, 3° 22.4′W.)

During the period from 1812 to 1833 Robert Stevenson was responsible for 18 new lights, including Dunnet Head. All of them were on large islands or Scotland's mainland, so he repeated a proven design. He delegated most of the day-to-day building to his assistant James Smith, a builder from Inverness. Smith had worked with Stevenson on Tarbat Ness, Lismore and Barra Head, so he was familiar with Stevenson's designs. The tower is white and stands 65 feet tall. The original light used reflectors, but in 1852 it was changed to a powerful lens. The light's current character flashes 4 white every 30 seconds and has a nominal range of 26 miles into the Pentland Firth.

A little bit more should be said about the Pentland Firth. The Firth is a channel, 6 to 8 miles wide and 14 miles long. Connecting the North Sea with the Atlantic Ocean, it separates the Scottish mainland from the Orkney Islands in a bewildering confusion of swirling eddies, tide races, counter currents and whirlpools. The Firth's rough waters have proven dangerous to small vessels since the spring tides run faster here than in almost any other body of water around Britain. The Merry Men of Mey, that forms on the ebb and is so turbulent that it can swallow up a small boat, is located on the western end of the Firth. On the eastern end are the Pentland Skerries, which can be extremely dangerous if the wind is against the tide. This treacherous body of water has cast stones through the lighthouse windows 346 feet above the waves. To make it even more dangerous, small islands also dot the Firth.

In contrast to the violence of the sea the natural beauty around the lighthouse is spectacular. Dunnet Bay, with its sweeping sands backed by dunes, provides a wealth of

Dunnet Head

interest for those who enjoy beautiful scenery and wildlife. The sands stretch for 2 miles south of the old sandstone cliffs of Dunnet Head and areas of active sand movement between the more stable grass-covered ridges are evident. Behind them lies a high ridge of dunes and, inland, blown sand has formed a machair-like area that constitutes part of the Dunnet Links National Nature Reserve.

The seashore and cliffs each provide habitats for a wide variety of flowering plants. You can find plump-leafed sea rocket and sea sandwort on a summer stroll, while on the rock platform and cliffs hardy thrift, scurvy grass and sea plantain cling to the rocks. In the open areas of Dunnet Forest and beside the pathways there are lime-loving plants alongside wetland plants of the ditches. In all, the Reserve boasts over 230 plant species. Rare butterflies, otters fishing amongst the kelp in the rocky bay, shy roe deer browsing in the forest or dunes, foxes at night or weasels can also be sighted.

The area is also a great place to gather seashells such as the tiny Groatie Buckie, regarded as lucky in Caithness, and the larger otter shell. Sea potatoes, sea urchins and mermaids' purses are also brought in by the tide.

The Visitor Centre and the Dunnet Links National Nature Reserve are off the A836 Thurso to John O'Groats road, about 15 minutes' drive from Thurso.

HOLBURN HEAD

David Stevenson, in his list of 45 possible sites needed to complete the system of lights for the coasts of Scotland after the Merchant Shipping Act of 1854, gave Scrabster on the west side of Thurso Harbour in Caithness as one of the priority sites. Holburn Head, the name given to the Scrabster light, was one of only two on Stevenson's list not selected without any reason given. This was only the beginning of Holburn Head's construction problems – it took four years to resolve a dispute over the access road to the station.

The lighthouse was finally established in 1862. As the engineer, David Stevenson built the station in the schoolhouse style with a 38-foot tower in the middle of the buildings.

Holburn Head

(Navigational location is 58° 36.9′N, 3° 32.4′W.) Like all of the lighthouses this station has gone through many changes. It was part of the Northern Lighthouse Board's electrification programme which converted the beacon in 1976. The white went to 9,500 candlepower, which gave it a range of 15 miles, and the red to 1,500 candlepower, giving it a range of 11 miles. This is still the current range of the light. The light's character is to flash white/red every 10 seconds.

Holburn Head was one of the Scottish lights bombed by the Germans during World War Two but was not damaged. A bigger danger now threatening the light is tentative plans to dredge Thurso Harbour. Holburn Head's buildings sit close to the shore and its road literally reaches the water's edge. Enlarging the harbour could mean the lighthouse would have to be destroyed.

The station was fully automated in 1988. Staff from Stroma and Cape Wrath occupied the keepers' accommodation until their facilities were automated. Today one of the keepers' houses has a long-term lease and the rest have been kept for Northern Lighthouse Board operations.

Nestled into the hillside of Thurso Bay, Holburn Head is one of the simplest Scottish lights to see. It can be easily viewed from the town of Thurso or is visible for miles from your car when travelling west on the A836. Scrabster is a major port for the P & O ferries to the Orkney Islands and you can get an excellent view of the spectacular lighthouse from on board the ferries.

The Scrabster area is well known for sea angling. West of Holburn Head is a point identifiable by the rock "nose" three-quarters of the way up the cliff. The sea angling boats use the depth change running out from the shelf because the big fish like the shelter. Tidal streams keep the flat bedrock clean.

Thurso Bay sweeps from Holburn Head in the west to Dunnet Head in the east. It has a fine harbour and the beach is recognised as the best surfing in the north, giving a wonderful panoramic view which includes the Orkney Island of Hoy.

There are many fossilized fish beds, representing deep lake phases, in the flagstones of northern Scotland, and Holburn Head fish bed is one of the best. Fossilized fish of the Middle Old Red Sandstone (Devonian period) of northern Scotland are preserved in finely coated, organic-rich siltstones that were deposited in the deep waters of a thermally layered

lake at Holburn. Preservation is excellent, with the finest details of external structure visible. The fish died en masse due to de-oxygenation events and salinity changes in the lake. The drifting carcasses sank into the deep waters of the lake (that contained no oxygen) where they were preserved. Work on the fish beds has shown that this deep lake phase lasted for 4,000 years during which time there were many changes in the fish species.

PENTLAND SKERRIES

In the days of sailing ships the narrow gap at the eastern end of the Pentland Firth was named "Hell's Mouth" by the awestruck sailors who had to sail through it. Located here are the Pentland Skerries, 4 miles south-east of Burwick on the Orkney Islands. (Position on the Nautical Chart is 58° 41.4′N, 2° 55.5′W.) The area is a small group of islets, stacks and reefs that include Muckle Skerry and a long shoal running north-east from Little Skerry to Clettack Skerry. Muckle Skerry has three tiny lochans and a table-shaped northern promontory called the "Tennis Court". The islet's population has fluctuated from 17 in 1881 to, more recently, only the lighthouse keepers. When the lighthouse was automated and the keepers removed in 1994 Muckle Skerry became deserted.

In order for ships not to have to take the long route around the Orkney Islands, two lighthouses were built in 1794 on Muckle Skerry to open up the Pentland Firth to shipping. The engineer for the lighthouses was Thomas Smith. One tower was 79 feet tall while the other was 59 feet tall, and the optics in both lighthouses used 66 reflectors. The lighthouses

Pentland Skerries

Pentland Skerries

were rebuilt in the 1820s in a more permanent form – the towers were made taller using stone from Herston and the larger tower was enlarged to over 100 feet. The optics were changed to refracting lenses in 1847 for higher efficiency. In 1895 the lower light was discontinued but the tower can still be seen, with a foghorn on top. Currently the Pentland Skerries has a character of flashing 3 white every 30 seconds.

The lighthouse service was run similarly to a military operation with a definite hierarchy. The Commissioners dictated that the principal keepers were "entitled to take the lead at all stations" and advised them to employ their authority with firmness but restraint. When some "loose notion" gained ground that assistants might dispute the authority of the principal, the Board stopped it quickly by fining three assistants at the Pentland Skerries.

Many Pentland Skerries lighthouse keepers have been commended for bravery. In 1871 Donald Montgomery, an assistant keeper, dived into raging waters to rescue a boy off the Wick fishing boat, *Good Desire*, which had gone ashore. Twelve men were rescued in 1884 from the *Vicksburgh of Leith* that was destroyed on the Skerries and the whole lighthouse crew was commended. In a thick fog in 1965 the 10,300-ton vessel, *Kathe Niederkirchner*, went ashore. The two assistant keepers climbed down the cliff and boarded the ship's lifeboat which was struggling in the dangerous waters. Taking charge, they guided the boat safe and sound to the lighthouse's east landing, bringing 50 crew and passengers ashore unharmed.

The keepers were put at risk during World War Two when the German air force strafed the lighthouse and hit the lantern and light room. Eleven windows were broken, twelve prisms were damaged, and thirteen bullet holes were found in the copper dome of the tower. The keepers had been in the light room only seconds before the attack.

You did not have to be a keeper on the Pentland Skerries to be famous. A donkey employed to carry stores from the boat-landing to the lighthouse before they had a tractor at the station became a celebrity of sorts. This animal seemed to know when the boat was due at the Skerries with supplies, often before the keepers did – the donkey would take off and hide in the most inaccessible part of the island a couple of hours before the boat was due to arrive.

ORKNEY

NORTH RONALDSAY

One of the first four lighthouses built by the Northern Lighthouse Board was on North Ronaldsay, the most remote of Orkney's North Isles. North Ronaldsay was selected because along with Sanday the island had caused many shipwrecks. The site chosen for the lighthouse was low-lying Kirk Taing and this low elevation required a tower 70 feet high. John White and James Sinclair were responsible for building this lighthouse according to a design by Thomas Smith – the facility, with catoptric or reflected optics, was established on 10 October 1789. In the early 1800s the light was removed and responsibility transferred to Start Point on Sanday, as 22 additional shipwrecks had occurred in this area after North Ronaldsay was lighted. The light also had problems with personnel.

Old lighthouse, North Ronaldsay

In 1854 a new light was built on North Ronaldsay about 500 yards west of what would become fondly known as the "old light". (Position on the Nautical Chart is 59° 23.4′N, 2° 22.8′W.) David and Thomas Stevenson were the engineers for the new facility. Due to the low-lying nature of North Ronaldsay the new tower made out of red brick with two white bands was 139 feet high making it Britain's tallest land-based lighthouse. The light flashes white every 10 seconds and has a range of 19 miles. The old light still stands, with a ball of masonry taken from Start Point replacing its lantern.

The lighthouse overlooks one of the strangest sheep farms in the world. North Ronaldsay still pursues the custom of common grazing on the seashore. There is little evidence of the true origin of North Ronaldsay's seaweed-eating sheep – bones dating from 3000 BC have been found to be "strikingly similar" to those of North Ronaldsay sheep, so the breed is thought to be 5,000 years old – they are black, brown, grey or white in colour. The tradition of grazing sheep on the island dates from the 18th century when a landowner decided that precious land was not to be wasted on the scraggy native sheep. He ordered local people to build a stone dyke around the island and the sheep were hustled outside the barrier to face the Atlantic on one side of the island and the North Sea on the other. The sheep, however, adapted and soon learned that the most exposed stretches of beach brought in the richest and tastiest deposits of seaweed.

New lighthouse, North Ronaldsay

There are about 2,000 of these sheep that live on a narrow strip of beach and foreshore outside the 13-mile stone dyke that surrounds the island. The sheep are brought inside the wall only at lambing and the island's sheep farmers herd them off the beaches into the stone-built "punds" for clipping and dipping. The act of punding is perhaps one of the last remaining elements of communal farming in Orkney.

Islanders talk with awe about the sheeps' strength in the water. "They're so strong that you're wasting your time trying to catch them. They swim out to the rocks and stand there laughing at you." This ability to evade capture is making it difficult for locals to expand a new trade – in Ronaldsay lamb. In the winter, when the tides bring in the best seaweed, the animals develop a flavour that is becoming popular with diners at some London restaurants.

North Ronaldsay was one of the last three lighthouses automated by the Northern Lighthouse Board on the evening of March 1998, along with the Butt of Lewis. The South Fair Isle Lighthouse followed suit at midnight to become the very last of the Scottish lights to be manned. A local trust will be developing the North Ronaldsay keepers' accommodation as a multi-purpose centre.

NOUP HEAD

Lying 25 miles from Kirkwall on the northern fringe of the Orkney Islands is Westray (West Island), the largest of the Orkney North Isles (11,646 acres), with a population of about 600. The island is known for its farmland, hilly moors, magnificent cliffs and sandy beaches. Beef cattle are the main contributor to the island's economy whose primary industries are agriculture and fishing, with tourism rapidly emerging as a strong third element in the island's monetary base. The Orkney straw-backed chairs are a Westray speciality, each one being handmade, numbered and distributed around the world. Westray is also the home port for Orkney's main fishing fleet.

There is much diversity in the scenery and Westray is often called the Queen of the North Isles. The cliffs are not as high as some other places on Orkney but are unusually

Noup Hea

Noup Head   beautiful. One of the favourites cliff areas is Noup Head. A peninsula which projects into the ocean and towers above the waves, the name Noup is derived from "gnupr", meaning high headland.

Sitting at the top of Noup Head on a rugged cliff face is the Noup Head Lighthouse, which along with Brough of Birsay protects shipping off Orkney's western seaboard. (Position on the Nautical Chart is 59° 19.9′N, 3° 04′W.) The light was established in 1898, and the engineer in charge was David A. Stevenson. Noup Head was the first lighthouse to use mercury flotation in the revolving carriage. The white tower stands 79 feet and the beacon flashes white every 30 seconds. The lighthouse was automated in 1964 and the keepers removed. The keepers' accommodation has been demolished and the station is being used for Northern Lighthouse Board operations.

Rising to 300 feet above sea level, Noup Head cliffs are a great place for birdwatching. These cliffs, stretching 4 miles south from the lighthouse, are a RSPB Reserve containing one of the largest seabird breeding grounds in Britain. Bird numbers are second only to remote St Kilda and huge numbers of nesting seabirds can be seen between April and July. Examples are fulmar, razorbill, kittiwake and shag, while the guillemot numbers are of international importance. A 1978 survey revealed over 40,000 guillemots, 1,200 razorbills, 1,000 fulmars and almost 25,000 pairs of kittiwakes. Peregrine falcons have been seen on the cliffs and ravens breed each year, raising their young in barbed-wire nests; there are also a few puffins. Most of the nesting seabirds have left their ledges by late July and all that are left are fulmars with their chicks.

The cliffs on the Westside near the lighthouse can be dangerous and should be approached with great care. You can find many caves, natural arches and interesting geos in

this area. Of particular note is the Gentleman's Cave in the cliffs south of Noup Head, which was once the hiding place of a number of Orkney lairds who supported the failed 1745 Jacobite rebellion. Westray islanders are said to have been the only Orcadians who supported the Jacobite cause after Culloden. Supporters for many years after the uprising would meet in the cave to drink the health of the "King of the Water".

The island can be reached by ferry on weekdays from Kirkwall and nearly islands.

HOY HIGH AND HOY LOW

A good example of the lighthouse concept known as "leading lights" can be found on the island of Graemsay. Leading lights are two lights that are located close together to give safer passage to ships going through a narrow body of water. The mariners use them to help "lead" their ships into port. If the captain keeps the lights in line with each other, the ship can avoid danger and pass safely. In this case the lights mark Hoy Sound, where powerful unstable waters known as "roosts" are common. In "roosts" the tide runs so fast that the surface of the sea forms high ridges with whirlpools in the channels between the ridges. The ridges move slowly but constantly, like sand dunes during a storm. Hoy Sound is the entrance to the port of Stromness and the naval anchorage of Scapa Flow, as well as important to fishermen – it became even more so with increased herring fishing in the 1900s.

The lights were established in 1851 so ships could clear the submerged Bow Rock of Hoy and the Kirk rocks of mainland Orkney on the western entrance of Scapa Flow. The engineer for this unique project was Alan Stevenson. Hoy Low is on the north-west of the island on the Taing of Oxan, and Hoy High is on the north-east of the island at Taing of

Hoy High

Sandside, next to the island's only bay, the Bay of Sandside, also known as the Hap. (Position on the Nautical Chart is 58° 56.5′N, 3° 18.4′W.) Hoy High has a white tower which is 115 feet tall – its light occults white/red every 8 seconds and has a nominal range of 20 miles. Hoy Low has a white tower of 40 feet and the character of the light is isophase white every 3 seconds. The stone to build the lighthouses were brought from Orkney's North Isles. Hoy High was automated in 1978 and Hoy Low in 1966. Both sets of accommodation now have private owners.

Hoy Low is doubly unique as a coastal battery and searchlights were built beside it during World War Two. At the start of the war, *HMS Royal Oak* was sunk by a German U47 submarine with the loss of 833 lives. Alarmed at the ease with which the Flow was penetrated, Winston Churchill ordered more blockships to be sunk and causeways to be constructed. Even though 1,700 men worked on them, The Churchill Barriers, as they are called, were not finished until spring 1945, when the war was almost over. Ships were sunk in order to block the channels between the four south Islands, Lamb Holm, Glimps Holm, Burray and South Ronaldsay, which gave access to Scapa Flow. It was believed that the

Hoy High

Churchill Barriers would be sufficient to render the channels unnavigable to enemy submarines and ships, and hence protect the British Grand Fleet in Scapa Flow. The two 6-pound batteries were no longer needed in Burray after the Churchill Barrier had been built. The Hoy lighthouses have a new duty since the war – they also help keep ships away from the Scapa Flow causeways that lead from mainland Orkney to the south islands.

Graemsay is a quiet place with a post office but no shop. The population is currently 23 and the island has a number of crofts but only one farm. Sandside Bay is a good spot for seal watching – over two hundred at a time have been counted during the breeding season. There are two early Celtic sites on Graemsay, one dedicated to St Bride and the other to St Columba. Walks over the top of the island upon ground untouched by plough or pesticides will reveal plenty of wild plants including orchids. It is particularly beautiful in the summer.

You can reach Graemsay on the passenger-only ferry, the Graemsay, that sails from Stromness pier to Moaness in North Hoy, calling at Graemsay.

Hoy Low

SHETLAND

MUCKLE FLUGGA

Located in the Burra Firth is the most northerly outpost in Britain. Farther north than Bergen in Norway, St Petersburg in Russia, Greenland's Cape Farewell and the Alaskan peninsula is the lighthouse of Muckle Flugga. (Position on the Nautical Chart is 60° 51.3′N,

Aerial view of Hoy

Muckle Flugga 0° 53′W,) The lighthouse sits at the top of a 200-foot rock just north of the Shetland Island of Unst and even located so high the station is constantly battered by surf. "The Flugga", as it is often called, was built in 1854 as a result of the Crimean War. A storm of near hurricane proportions in 1811 sunk the 98-gun *St George* and the 74-gun *Defence in the Baltic* with the loss of 2,000 lives, twice as many deaths as at the Battle of Trafalgar. The Admiralty felt that one of the obvious dangers was the unlit state of the north and east coast of the Shetland Islands, since the Royal Navy would pass here on its way to blockade Russia's northern ports.

The need was established but it took a long time for the Northern Lighthouse Board, The Elder Brethren of Trinity House and the Board of Trade to come to agreement on the building of the light on Muckle Flugga. David Stevenson was sent north in March 1854 by the Northern Lighthouse Board to find a suitable place for the lighthouse. He was unable to land on the island and so he returned home reporting that it was completely impractical to build a lighthouse in such a place. Three months later a committee of Elder Brethren from Trinity visited Unst on a fine day and rowed out to Muckle Flugga on a quiet sea. The two lighthouse authorities avoided a major confrontation because of the need for the lighthouse. The Board sent another inspection team and it was decided that erecting and maintaining a temporary light was possible.

N

Because of the war a 22-foot tower with a cast-iron lantern on top and temporary accommodation were constructed. The light was surrounded by a casing of rubble set in cement and was turned on for the first time on 11 October 1854. David Stevenson's predictions came true when winter storms battered the new lighthouse with flooding occurring in the kitchen and spray breaking over the summit of the tower. Stevenson went to London where he told the Board of Trade of the terrible conditions at the "The Flugga" and stated that "life is in jeopardy". The Board of Trade still felt the light was vital. A compromise was reached by approving Stevenson to build a stronger and more permanent station for the keepers.

The construction of a permanent light was begun in 1856 and the engineers for the project were Thomas and David Stevenson. It was the first lighthouse in such an exposed location to be made of brick – one of the main reasons being that it was easier to transport bricks onto the island. This seemed to work as the 64-foot white tower was completed and the light was turned on for the first time on 1 January 1858. The beacon currently flashes 2 white every 20 seconds and has a range of 25 miles.

Due to the wildness of the location a shore station was established on Burra Firth at the north end of Unst. *The Grace Darling*, the lighthouse tending boat, along with the boatman, was also based at Burra Firth. The boat was replaced with a helicopter and the station automated in 1995.

Shore Station at Burra Firth

After automation the shore station was sold. The principal keeper's flat has been taken over by the Scottish National Heritage and transformed into an informative visitor centre for Herma Ness Reserve. The Northern Lighthouse Board kept the offshore lighthouse complex for operations.

To visit Muckle Flugga one must fly or take a ferry to Lerwick in Shetland, from where one can go by car or bus to Unst. The trip includes two "roll-on roll-off" ferry crossings. Once reaching Herma Ness it is a long walk to the shore where there is a good view of the lighthouse.

ESHANESS

A temporary light powerful enough to give warning of the Ve Skerries eight and half miles offshore was erected in 1915 on the Eshaness peninsula on the north-west coast of mainland Shetland. The light was an iron tower, containing a lantern, machinery and an acetylene generating plant, and was constructed in about two months. The building materials reached the remote location by pony and cart once they arrived on the Shetland Islands. The temporary light was torn down after World War One.

The current Eshaness Lighthouse was built in 1929. (Position on the Nautical Chart is 60° 29.3′N, 1° 37.6′W.) It was the last Northern Lighthouse Board manned facility designed by a member of the Stevenson family, David A. Stevenson being the engineer for the station.

The 37-foot square tower sits on top of a 200-foot cliff. The beacon flashes white every 12 seconds and in 1974 the candlepower was increased to 46,500 to give the light a nominal range of 25 miles. The small house was home to only one keeper, which was unusual in that most manned facilities had three keepers.

At Stenness, the site of a former fishing station sheltered by Stenness Isle, is a stone cross erected by the Commissioners for Northern Lighthouses in 1927, to mark the spot where supplies for the Eshaness Lighthouse were landed.

Eshaness did not prove to be totally effective in keeping ships away from the Ve Skerries. The Aberdeen trawler *Ben Doran* was wrecked in the area soon after the lighthouse was built and all hands were lost. Due to heavy oil-tanker traffic bound to and from Sullom Voe, a lighthouse was built on the Ve Skerries in 1979. Eshaness was used as the construction site for the Ve Skerries light.

The station was automated in 1974 and sold to a private owner. It has been sold twice since then and my husband and I bought Eshaness in 1999. Our house was completely renovated by the previous owners to match the style of the original lighthouse keeper's accommodation. The house looks much like it would have when David A. Stevenson built it, with the exception of the kitchen which has all modern appliances.

The question everyone seems to ask is: "What is it like to live in a Scottish lighthouse accommodation?" My first response is that it feels safe with 3-foot-thick walls and shutters on both the inside and outside windows to protect us from the violent storms which plague the area. One of the biggest challenges of living at Eshaness is trying to keep up with the weather as a single day can present all seasons. We have come to cherish calm days, as Eshaness is a windy place most of the time.

Eshaness

If there is a disadvantage to living in this historical building it is tourists. Our "backyard" is the world-famous Eshaness Cliffs, which have been designated a national seashore area, so we have many visitors. Most of them just take a picture of the cliffs and lighthouse and leave, which is fine. Some, however, do not respect our "Private House" sign. We will find them wandering inside our fence or looking in the window. There is so much to see in the area that if they went for a walk, within a short distance they would find puffins, seals, red-throated divers, Arctic terns, gannets and many wild flowers.

The big advantage to living at a Scottish lighthouse station today is that the tower is maintained and kept operational. Like all of the Northern Lighthouse Board automated facilities, we have an attendant who makes sure the light sweeps by our windows every night right on schedule.

SUMBURGH

At the southern end of "mainland" Shetland lays the turbulent stretch of water known as "Sumburgh Roost" where tides and waves battle whenever the winds are high. In order to avoid the dangers of the Pentland Firth large ships of 1,200 to 1,400 tons went through the

Sumburgh passage on their trip from Sweden to Australia. A light was needed to protect ships in this treacherous area so Sumburgh Head Lighthouse was established in 1821, becoming the first lighthouse built in the Shetland Islands. (Position on the Nautical Chart is 59° 51.3′N, 1° 16.3′W.) The engineer for the project was Robert Stevenson and the builder was John Reid of Peterhead who chose to have walls of double thickness to keep out the dampness. The original beacon had 26 reflectors around the light – the beacon's character now is to flash 3 white every 30 seconds.

Sumburgh Head Lighthouse was rocked with scandal in 1871 when a "conspiracy" occurred among the keepers. Two keepers were dismissed, including the principal keeper with 23 years of service, after they agreed to not report the other for sleeping at his post. Falling asleep on watch was the most serious offence a keeper could commit. Failure to check the light might allow the revolving machinery to run down which would alter its character or even allow it to go out.

The lighthouse was automated in 1991 and the keepers' accommodation has become a self-catering operation. It is a popular destination for holidaymakers as it is easy to reach from bustling Sumburgh Airport. The area directly around the lighthouse is a RSPB reserve and an interpretive board gives information on the impressive seabird colony – the area is especially well known for its puffins. The Royal Society for the Protection of Birds also has its Shetland office in one of the lighthouse keeper's cottages. The Scottish Natural Heritage has declared the cliffs at Sumburgh Head a Site of Special Scientific Interest as well as a Special Protection Area of International Importance. The Shetland Islands, lying close to the edge of the European continental shelf and encircled by the waters of the North Atlantic, are amongst the finest areas to see whales and dolphins in the entire British Isles. It is not unusual to see both off Sumburgh Head.

Near the lighthouse is St Ninian's Isle which was once tidal. At present, vehicles are not permitted to drive on the private road to the beach and tombolo. It is an easy walk crossing the beautiful tombolo of shell sand, one of the best examples of its type in Europe,

Sumburgh

Sumburgh

although in severe tides boots may be needed to cross. The island was populated until 1700 when the peat supply ran out. In 1958 a local schoolboy discovered a cache of Pictish silver on the island in the remains of the 12th-century church. The 28 objects were buried in a larch box and unearthed during excavations. It is believed that the Vikings built the church in 1150 on an earlier site. Replicas of the silver can be seen in the Shetland Museum as the real silver now resides in the Royal Scottish Museum in Edinburgh.

A former laird's house near the lighthouse was made into the Sumburgh Hotel. A two-minute walk from the hotel is the historic site of Jarlshof, which emerged after a gale in the late 19th century. The site dates back 3,000 years and is many-layered, with settlements from Neolithic dwellings to a 16th-century laird's house. There is an interpretive centre and both children and adults will enjoy exploring the ruins.

FAIR ISLE NORTH and FAIR ISLE SOUTH

Fair Isle is midway between Orkney and Shetland about 24 miles south-west of Shetland. It is often called the "Island of Sheep" and is famed for its knitwear and birds. Only three miles long by one and a half miles wide, the island is surrounded by impressive red sandstone cliffs, rising to over 328 feet at spectacular Sheep Rock and to almost 650 feet along the heavily indented west coast. The majority of the inhabitants live in the south where there is a limited amount of ground for cultivation. The National Trust for Scotland owns the island. In the mid 19th century 380 folk lived there, yet a century later it supported less than 50. The population increased to 67 in 1991 and much has been done to improve conditions on individual properties and the island as a whole.

The population took a small drop at the end of March 1998 when Fair Isle South Lighthouse had its keepers removed. The last of the Northern Lighthouse Board's lights had been automated – the end of a long tradition of manned lighthouses in Scotland. Now there are no keepers in the Northern Lighthouse Board system, only attendants who visit the lights on a periodic basis to make sure the computer and all the mechanisms are working correctly. Some feel this was a sad occurrence but with new technology the keeper's job had radically changed. As one keeper told me, at the end they mainly just painted and kept the property in tip-top shape.

Fair Isle North

Fair Isle has two lighthouses built in 1892 with the engineer for both projects being David A. Stevenson – Fair Isle North (position on the Nautical Chart is 59° 33.2′N, 1° 36.5′W) and Fair Isle South (position on the Nautical Chart is 59° 30.9′N, 1° 39′W). Fair Isle North has a 46-foot white tower and the light's character is flashing 2 white every 30 seconds with a nominal range of 22 miles. Fair Isle South has a white tower that is 85 feet tall. Its beacon has a range of 24 miles and its character is 4 white flashes every 30 seconds. The North Lighthouse was automated in 1981, the keepers' accommodation demolished and the rest of the station kept for Northern Lighthouse Board operations. National Trust for Scotland will use the Fair Isle South accommodation as a multi-purpose centre.

When the keepers were still in charge, the closeness of the two lighthouses led to a keen inter-light competition. At first it was a monthly two-legged sport contest for the Fair Isle Light Keepers' Trophy, a cheap plastic cup painted silver. At the North Light they would compete in darts. A couple of days later they would then go to the South Light for a golf

Fair Isle South

tournament where the keepers had built a six-hole golf course. Not having all the necessary equipment to build the course the keepers used steamed-pudding tins for holes and broom handles with red flags on them for markers.

During World War Two both lighthouses came under attack from enemy aircraft. In 1941 the outbuildings of the North Light were bombed and demolished by a direct hit. The wife of assistant keeper Sutherland was killed standing at her kitchen window in the same raid by a bomb blast. Six weeks later the enemy planes returned to target the South Light. A direct hit on the lighthouse keepers' accommodation claimed the lives of the principal keeper's wife and daughter. The lighthouse itself was severely damaged and a soldier manning a machine gun at the lighthouse killed. Robert Macauley, one of the North Lighthouse keepers, accompanied by his daughter, walked through a gale and 3-foot snow drifts to help the badly damaged South Light get in condition to operate that night. He then walked back in the dark and snow to man the North Light.

Bell Rock

EAST COAST

BELL ROCK

One of the greatest achievements of Robert Stevenson's tenure as engineer for the Northern Lighthouse Board was the design and overseeing of the building of a lighthouse on Inchcape Rock situated in the northern reaches of the Firth of Forth, lying directly in the way of shipping approaching the River Tay and the Dundee. (Position on the Nautical Chart is 56° 26.1′N, 2° 23.1′W.) The name chosen for the lighthouse was Bell Rock, which comes from a legend that claims that in olden times a bell attached to a tree was put on the rock by an abbot and that it rang continuously, being moved by the sea, to signify danger and warn ships.

The rock on which the lighthouse was built is only 131 feet long and 230 feet wide, surrounded by a dangerous reef which extends to three times that length and is twice as wide, making access difficult. The major building problem was that the higher part of the rock was barely uncovered at low tide. The solid part of the building is 13 feet above high water and the lowest part is sloped so that it is less likely to obstruct waves. The tower Stevenson designed was made of stone similar to the famous Eddystone Light. Bell Rock's tower is nearly 33 feet higher, reaching some 115 feet. Construction began in 1807 with teams of skilled workmen, but that year only 14 ten-hour days were available for building to take place between the tides. In 1808, from May to September, there were a total of only 22 such days.

The light's foundations consist of 400 stones, totalling about 388 tons, which were cut to fit into the inconsistencies of the rock base. They were joined by a specially prepared Bell Rock mortar, dovetailed together and secured above and below by small stone joggles. The foundation stones were completed on 10 July and were blessed with a benediction, three cheers and a toast to the future. During 1809 and 1810 the rest of the stones were put in place. Near the top of the tower the walls gradually narrow to allow for six rooms, 10 feet in diameter, for the machinery and crew. In all, 2,835 stones were used in the construction of the lighthouse and the total weight of masonry, the lantern and its apparatus is 2,083 tons.

Bell Rock

The light currently has a nominal range of 28 miles and flashes white every 5 seconds. It was fully automated on the 26 October 1988 and is currently used for Northern Lighthouse Board operations.

Stevenson was deeply impressed by the devotion of the work crews and his account of building the lighthouse is often called the "the Robinson Crusoe of civil engineering". Typical of the spirit that pervaded Bell Rock's construction, and public interest in it, was the ceremony of carting the last stone to Leith. The stone with a flag fixed on it, the masons in new aprons, the seamen and the Bell Rock carters with ribbons in their hats, and even the "faithful" and trusty horse "Brassy" decked with bows and coloured streamers made an impressive procession. When they passed the Trinity House of Leith, long interested in the lighting of Bell Rock, their officer appeared in uniform with his staff of office. At the harbour where the tending boat Seaton lay, the other ships hoisted their colours in salute.

On 1 February 1811 mariners were informed that the light on the Bell Rock would shine out "from the going away of daylight in the evening until the return of daylight in the morning". Bell Rock beacon was the first coloured light in the Northern Lighthouse Board service producing red and white beams.

From the beginning three men were on duty. They were paid more than other keepers not only because they were on a rock station, but also because they had among their duties the training of new keepers. The station needed a tender assigned to it, which also brought up the cost of the operation. Due to the high construction and maintenance costs, the ships passing Bell Rock had to pay double the duty of other lighthouses.

During the World Wars, Bell Rock was in jeopardy many times. In October 1915 a 650-man ship was totally destroyed on Bell Rock within 420 feet of the base of the tower, with no loss of life involved. During World War Two a German plane machine-gunned the tower breaking the lantern glass and "frosting" some lens prisms. Another time a German bomb exploded within ten yards of the tower but Stevenson's masterpiece still stood.

Bass Rock

BASS ROCK

Bass Rock is a small, 19-acre rock off the east coast of mainland Scotland near North Berwick. It is a volcanic plug of phonolite rock that rises 350 feet in the air. The island has a long history. Originally the rock belonged to the Bishopric of St Andrews but the Lauders family was granted the island by Malcolm Canmore in 1056. It has through the centuries been used as a hiding place – Prince James, later to become James I, hid there in 1405 and the church records from Dunbar were hidden there. In the 1600s the rock was used to imprison disobedient Covenanters. After the Battle of Killiecrankie, Bass Rock was the lone Jacobite strong-hold showing that not all Britain was Hanoverian – a handful of desperate men held out for four years under the rock's pro-Stuart governor,

Bass Rock

Charles Maitland. In 1694, William of Orange dispatched two warships, aided by smaller vessels, which cut off all supplies to the rock and the little garrison surrendered in April. They had saved some bottles of the best French wine and these, along with some fine biscuits, led the Commissioners to believe that they had provisions for years to come. The 16 rebels were able to negotiate good terms and were finally granted an amnesty. In 1706 the fortress was torn down and Sir Hew Dalrymple became the island's owner. He used the island to graze sheep and collect gannets to eat.

In 1902 Bass Rock Lighthouse was established. (Position on the Nautical Chart is 56° 4.6′N, 2° 38.3′W.) Building the station on a sheer-sided 300-foot-high rock with one landing place was no easy task for the engineer, David A. Stevenson. The best site was on the gun platform of the old fortress. An attempt was made to begin building there, but part of the old fortress fell in so the retaining wall had to be rebuilt. The 65-foot white tower clings precariously to the side of the rock 150 feet above the sea. The beacon, flashing 3 white every 20 seconds, has a range of about 21 miles into the Firth of Forth and North Sea.

A time came when the only human inhabitants on the island were the lighthouse keepers, though many ornithologists came to the island to study the main inhabitants – gannets. Seven per cent of the world's gannet population are hatched on this little rock. When the lighthouse keepers were removed during World War Two the gannets became the lighthouse's temporary keepers as they were found nesting in the buildings along with a cormorant that was bringing up her young in a coal bunker. When the keepers were removed after automation in 1988 the gannets again ruled the island. The lighthouse property was not sold but is being utilized for Northern Lighthouse Board operations.

The only way to visit Bass Rock is by ship from North Berwick during the summer months and the boat trip is a unique experience. A huge cave 32 feet high and 557 feet long cuts through the base of the rock from east to west. Seals are often seen swimming in the cave and, if the weather is calm, visitors can go through it in a dinghy. The views of the

Buchan Ness

lighthouse are remarkable, even though they are often obstructed by thousands of seabirds soaring and diving. The noise is deafening with the cries of birds and the sea crashing in the cave and the rocky clefts. The largest impact is made by the smell of the island. It is covered with guano from thousands of birds and many find this off-putting.

BUCHAN NESS

The most easterly point of Scotland is a small island called Buchan Ness. The village of Boddam just south of Peterhead is a fishing village built of granite sitting above a harbour with massive concrete walls. A small footbridge that is under water at high tide connects the village to a one-acre island whose only building is Buchan Ness Lighthouse. (Position on the Nautical Chart is 57° 28.2′N, 1° 46.4′W.)

The lighthouse was built in 1827 with Robert Stevenson as engineer and John Gibb of Aberdeen as contractor. In 1825 Stevenson proposed to the Board in his report that the new Fresnel system be adopted in the facility but the new system was not used at Buchan Ness, reflectors being used instead. However, Buchan Ness was the first station to have a flashing light. Currently the beacon flashes white every 5 seconds and has a range of 28 miles. During the 1870s Sir William Thompson hailed Buchan Ness along with two other lights as one of "undoubtedly the three best revolving lights in the world". In 1910 Buchan Ness was converted to the dioptric system and the lantern was enlarged with candlepower being raised from 6,500 to 786,000. In 1978 the candlepower was again raised to 2,000,000. The Buchan Ness tower, built of granite and brick, is 115 feet tall. In 1907, a distinctive red band was added around its middle as a day mark.

During World War Two Buchan Ness Lighthouse was under attack not from aeroplanes but from mines. Drifting mines were blown onto the rocky shores of the island and exploded on two occasions. None of the lighthouse personnel were injured but it was a frightening time.

In fact through history the biggest problem for the lighthouse has been being so close to Boddam. Two keepers lost their jobs for visiting the pub too often. In 1996 the lighthouse foghorn made the news for having disturbed the village residents for ninety years. The story came to light when a boy in the village who was suffering from leukaemia could not get enough rest after his treatment every two weeks. A request was made that the foghorn be turned off, supported by the entire village, including the fishermen whom the horn was supposed to protect.

Buchan Ness was automated in 1988, the keepers removed and their accommodation sold. In January 2000 the property was once again up for sale. The news report said:

The lighthouse at Buchan Ness, a rocky outcrop on the Aberdeenshire coast, south of Peterhead, is one of the more unusual homes for sale at the moment. Accessed by a bridge, which is under water at high tide and with its own helicopter pad, it is frequently battered by strong winds from the North Sea. And when there is a thick mist, the foghorn sounds out to warn off ships out at sea. The unique property has given rise to a lot of interest, despite a price tag of over £200,000 [US $330,000].

Evidently there was not enough interest as the sale was withdrawn.

GLOSSARY

Acetylene – A gas derived from water and calcium carbide used in lighthouses after the 1920s. It was the first fuel to eliminate the need for a keeper to carry oil up the tower.

Argand Reflector – A variety of light used in lighthouses that featured a hollow wick in a glass chimney with a silvered parabolic reflector behind to intensify the light. The Argand reflector lamp was named after Aimé Argand, the Swiss inventor who developed the design.

Breakwater – A pier built across the mouth of a harbour to slow down the sea moving towards the harbour.

Catadioptric – Used both methods of magnification (catoptric and dioptric). A prism can both reflect and refract, depending upon the angle at which the light falls upon the surface of the glass, while a lens usually only refracts. Using a complex combination of prisms and lenses, a very intense and highly magnified beam of light can be created.

Catoptric – The catoptric system involves using a parabolic reflector behind the light, which is often spun around the light to produce the rotating flash one usually associates with lighthouses. The catoptric system is similar to that used in modern flashlights; if you take one apart you'll see a parabolic reflector in which the lightbulb is the focal point.

Catwalk – A narrow elevated walkway allowing the keeper access to light towers built out in the water.

Character of the Light – Means of identifying lighthouses by their method of flashing.

Dalén – Regulates a gaslight source by the action of sunlight, turning it off at dawn and on at dusk or at other periods of darkness.

Day Mark – A unique colour, pattern or architecture of towers and other markers used by navigators to mark their location during the day.

Dioptric – Used a Fresnel lens to concentrate the light. Fresnel lenses take a point of light (such as a lightbulb) and force the light forward in one direction.

Draught – The depth of water necessary to float a ship.

Fixed Light – A steady, non-flashing beam.

Flashing – The light is off for longer than it is on.

Focal Plane – The level plane at which the lighthouse or leading light's lens is focused; the height of this plane is measured from mean sea level.

Fog Signal – Any type of audible device that could warn mariners of obstacles during periods of heavy fog when the light could not be seen. Bells, whistles and horns, either manually or power operated were all used with varying degrees of success.

Fresnel Lens – A system of angular prisms that refract and reflect light into a beam. Invented in 1821 by Augustin Fresnel, this system captures and focuses up to 70 per cent of the light emitted from the illuminant. Fresnel designed a variety of lens system sizes that he defined by orders. The first-order lens is the largest and is typically used in coastal lights. The sizes of the lenses and their effective range decrease as the order number increases.

Gallery – Outdoor railed walkway encircling the watch room where the keeper sat and monitored the lantern and weather conditions.

GPS – An electronic system for identifying positions, GPS is an acronym for Global Positioning System. A GPS receiver decodes a satellite's coded signals to calculate its position.

Holophotal – Means "whole light" in Greek.

Inner Leading Light – The light in a pair of leading lights that is situated behind the other as viewed from the water.

Island Lighthouse – Built on a small island a short distance from the shore.

Lamp – The oil-lighting apparatus inside a lens. A lamp was used before electricity powered the illuminant.

Lantern – The portion of the lighthouse structure that houses and protects the lens and illuminant; its relative size is described and defined by the size of the lens, often based on the seven Fresnel orders. Also referred to as the lantern room.

Lantern Glass – Glass panes in the lantern that protect the lens and illuminant while allowing the maximum amount of light to pass. Also referred to as "lantern glazing".

Lantern Room – A room surrounded by windows which housed the lighthouse lens.

Leading Lights – A pair of lights placed in such a manner that when they are visually lined up one behind the other, they lead a vessel into harbour. Another term used for these lights is "Range Lights".

Lens – Any glass or transparent material that is shaped to focus light.

Lewis Lamp – A variety of light that used a silvered copper reflector behind a glass lens. The design of the Lewis Lamp was heavily "borrowed" from that of the Argand Reflector, and was named after Winslow Lewis who imported the design from Europe.

Lighthouse Tender – Ship used to supply the light and fog signal stations, maintain buoys and service lightships. Today, similar vessels are called buoy tenders.

Lightship – A moored vessel that marked a harbour entrance or a dangerous projection such as a reef where lighthouses could not be constructed.

Light Station – Refers not only to the lighthouse but to all the buildings at the installation supporting the lighthouse, including keepers' quarters, oil house, fog signal building, cisterns, boathouse, workshop, etc. Some light stations have had more than one lighthouse over the years.

LORAN – An electronic system for identifying position. LORAN is an acronym for Long-Range Radio Navigation. A LORAN receiver measures the differences in the arrival of signals from three or more transmitters to calculate its position.

Major Light – Has a range of over 15 nautical miles.

Minor Light – Has a range of less than 15 nautical miles.

Nominal Range – The distance at which a lighthouse is visible – this depends on its height when light intensity and other factors are considered equal.

Occulting – The light is usually on for longer periods of time than it is off.

Oil House – A small building, usually made of stone or concrete, which stored oil for lighthouse lamps. Oil houses were built after paraffin, a highly flammable agent, came into use as an illuminant.

Oil Vapour Lamp – A variety of lamp in which oil is forced into a vaporizing chamber, and then into a mantle. It is similar to the Coleman Lamps used in camping today.

Optic – Revolving a beam of light in a circle at a given rotation gives the impression to an observer that the light is flashing, whilst in fact the light is on constantly. It is not the source of the light that rotates, but the apparatus (known as the optic) that creates the beam.

Outer Leading Light – The light in a pair of leading lights that is situated in front of the other as viewed from the water.

Parabolic – A bowl-shaped reflector in which sections which are parallel to the plane of symmetry are always an equal distance from the source.

Parapet – A walkway with railings which encircled the lamp room.

Pier – A structure extending into navigable waters for use as a landing place, or to protect or form a harbour.

Range Lights – Another name for leading lights.

Refraction – When a ray of light passes through a material (such as glass) it is bent as it does so. Fresnel, a Frenchman, discovered the effect in 1822. Prisms of glass, when arranged in certain ways, can be made to greatly magnify light, so long as the light is at the focal point.

Rock Lighthouses – Built on a small rock in the middle of the sea. Accommodation was limited and the keepers lived in just a few tiny rooms. They slept in a single bedroom in curved bunks known as banana bunks, around the curvature of the tower. Keepers' families lived on the mainland in shore stations. The keepers operated in two teams of three, working one month on duty and one month off duty.

Screwpile – A type of piling fitted with a helical fluke that is twisted into the bottom of a body of water, and a type of lighthouse employing screwpilings as its primary foundation system.

Shoal – A shallow area, such as a sandbar or rock formation.

Shore or Land Lighthouse – Lighthouses usually built on headlands and where accommodation was usually large enough to allow the keepers to live with their families.

Shore Station – Where the families of keepers from rock or island lights lived. Sometimes the keepers' families lived on the island; sometimes they lived in a shore station. Keepers with families at shore stations rotated their schedules.

Ventilation Ball – The perforated spherical ball at the apex of the lantern roof that originally provided ventilation for the oil-fired illuminant.

Watch Room – A room, usually located immediately beneath the lantern room, fitted with windows through which a lighthouse keeper could observe water conditions during storm periods.

Wickies – A nickname give to early lighthouse keepers who spent a great deal of their time trimming the wick on the lamp in order to keep it burning brightly and to minimizesooting.

BIBLIOGRAPHY

Allardyce, Keith, *Scotland's Edge Revisited*. HarperCollins, 1998
ISBN: 000472194

Allardyce, Keith, and Hood, Evelyn, *At Scotland's Edge*. HarperCollins, 1996
ISBN: 0004356608

Bathurst, Bella, *The Lighthouse Stevenson*. HarperCollins, 1999
ISBN: 0002570068

Grant, Kay, *Robert Stevenson – Engineer and Sea Builder*. Meredith Press, 1969
Library Congress Catalog Number: 69 19046

Munro, R.W., *Scottish Lighthouses*. Thule Press, 1979
ISBN: 0906191327

Krauskopf, Sharma, *Scotland – The Complete Guide*. Appletree Press, 1999
ISBN: 0862817552

Krauskopf, Sharma, *Scotland – The Complete Guide and Road Atlas*. The Globe Pequot Press, 1999
ISBN: 0762705817

Scott, Sir Walter, *The Voyage of the Pharos – Walter Scott's Cruise Around Scotland in 1814*. Scottish Library Association, 1998
ISBN: 0900649461

INDEX

A

Aberdeen 13, 14, 15, 72, 82
Ailsa Craig 16, 26, 28
Alan Stevenson 19, 24, 51, 67
Ardnamurchan 4, 11, 15, 21, 50, 51, 52
Argyll 13, 14, 50, 52
Arran 26, 28
Auskerry 16, 22

B

Barns Ness 16, 23
Barra Head 10, 15, 20, 56
Bass Rock 5, 12, 16, 80, 81
Bell Rock 5, 6, 12, 15, 20, 22, 23, 28, 37, 38, 78, 79, 80
Bressay 16, 22
British Open 26
Buchan Ness 5, 12, 15, 20, 36, 82, 83
Burra Firth 69, 71
Bute 13, 14
Butt of Lewis 4, 10, 16, 22, 44, 45, 46, 64

C

Cairnryan 28, 29
Caithness 11, 13, 58
Caledonian MacBrayne 40
Calf of Man 15, 17, 20
Campbeltown 10, 13, 31, 32, 34
Cantick Head 15, 22
Cape Wrath 4, 11, 15, 20, 24, 25, 46, 54, 55, 56, 59
Catadioptric 84
Catoptric 63, 84
Celts 8, 12
Chanonry 15
Chicken Rock 16, 22
Clyde 12, 13, 28, 32, 33
Clythness 17, 23
Colonsay 16
Commissioners for Irish Lights 13
Copinsay 17, 23
Corran 45
Corsewall Point 4, 10, 20, 27, 28

Covesea Skerries 15, 21
Crimean Canal 10
Crimean War 22, 70
Cromarty 15, 21

D

Dalén 41, 84
Davaar 15, 22
David Stevenson 21, 23, 24, 41, 44, 52, 53, 58, 71
Department of Trade 44, 45, 46
Douglas Head 16, 22
Draught 41, 84
Dubh Artach 16, 22, 23, 40
Duncansby Head 7, 17, 19, 23
Dundee 12, 20, 23, 78
Dunnet Bay 56
Dunnet Head 5, 11, 15, 20, 56, 58, 59
Dunskirkloch 29

E

Edinburgh 8, 12, 13, 17, 19, 20, 21, 23, 24, 41, 45, 49, 76
Eigg 43, 50
Eilean Glas 13, 14, 19
Eshaness 5, 12, 17, 23, 72, 74

F

Fair Isle North 5, 12, 16, 76, 77
Fair Isle South 5, 16, 76, 77
Fethaland 17
Fidra 16
Fife Ness 17
Firth of Forth 14, 15, 16, 78, 81
Fladda 16, 22
Flannan Isle 4, 10, 16, 23, 25, 40, 46, 49
Fresnel lens 7, 21, 23, 38, 84, 85

G

Gairloch 53
Galloway 4, 9, 10, 15, 20, 28, 29, 55
George Dempster 13
Gigha 10
Girdle Ness 15, 20
Glasgow Airport 26
Graemsay 11, 15, 67, 69

Guillemots 30, 55, 56, 66
Gulf Stream 9

H

Harvie 32
Hebrides 4, 10, 14, 15, 16, 17, 35
Helliar Holm 16, 23
Highlands 9
Holburn Head 5, 11, 16, 22, 58, 59
Holophotal 23, 85
Holy Island Inner 16, 22
Holy Isle Outer 17, 23
Hoy High 11, 21, 67, 68
Hoy Low 11, 67, 68
Hyskeir 10, 16, 23, 38, 39, 40
Hyslop 24

I

Inchkeith 14, 20
Inverness 13, 14, 56
Irish Sea 29
island of Barra 15
Islay 10, 15, 16, 20, 35, 36, 37
Isle of Lewis 15, 16, 46, 53, 55
Isle of Man 13, 14, 15, 16, 17, 24, 28, 30
Isle of Mull 14
Isle of Ornsay 10, 41, 42
Isle of Orsay 35
Isle of Skye 15, 41

J

J.D. Gardner 24
James Maxwell 12
Jarlshof 76
John Oswald 24
John Rennie 20
John Williamson 24
Jura 10, 16

K

Killantringan 16
Kinnaird Head 13, 14, 19, 20
Kintyre 6, 9, 10, 13, 14, 15, 19, 20, 21, 28, 30, 31, 32, 33, 35
Kirkcudbright Bay 15

Kirkwall 64, 67
kittiwakes 30, 55, 66
Kyle of Durness 56
Kyleakin 15, 22, 42

L

Lanark 13
Langness 16, 22
Leading lights 23, 67, 85, 86, 87
Lismore 15, 20, 56
Little Cumbrae 13
Little Minch 10, 38, 40, 51
Loch Ewe 53, 54
Loch Linnhe 16
Loch Ryan 15, 21, 28, 29

M

Maughold Head 17, 23
Maxwell, Gavin 40, 42
McArthur's Head 16, 22, 35, 45
Melvaig 53, 54
Merchant Shipping Act of 1854 41, 58
Merchant Shipping Act of 1894 14
Merchant Shipping Act of 1995 14
Merchant Shipping and Maritime Security Act 1997 14
Merry Men of Mey 56
Monach 16, 17, 22
Moray Firth 15
Muck 50
Muckle Flugga 12, 15, 22, 69, 70, 72
Muckle Skerry 61
Mull of Galloway 10, 15, 20, 29
Mull of Kintyre 6, 10, 13, 14, 19, 20, 21, 30, 32, 33, 35

N

Neist Point 6, 10, 17, 23, 40, 41
North Atlantic Drift 9, 12
North Carr 16
North Ronaldsay 11, 13, 14, 15, 19, 22, 63, 64
North Sea 9, 11, 15, 20, 23, 56, 63, 81, 83
North Uist 16
Northern Lighthouse Board 6, 7, 12, 13, 14, 17, 18, 19, 20, 21, 22, 23, 24, 30, 32, 33, 34, 35, 37, 39, 40, 41, 49, 51, 52, 54, 59, 63, 64, 66, 70, 72, 74, 76, 77, 78, 79, 80, 81
Noss Head 15, 18, 21
Noup Head 11, 16, 23, 64, 66, 67

O

Old Man of Stoer 52
Orkney 11, 12, 13, 14, 15, 16, 25, 56, 59, 61, 63, 64, 66, 67, 68, 69, 76
Orsay 36
Out Skerries 15, 22
Outer Hebrides 10, 14, 15, 165

P

Parabolic 13, 37, 84, 87
Pentland Firth 11, 14, 16, 55, 56, 61, 74
Pentland Skerries 11, 14, 56, 61, 62
Peregrine falcons 66
Peterhead 75, 82, 83
Picts 8
Pladda 14, 45
Point of Ayre 15, 20
Portnahaven 35, 36
Prestwick Airport 26
Puffins 7, 30, 55, 56, 66, 74, 75

R

Rattray Head 16, 23
Razorbills 30, 55, 66
Renfrew 13
Rhum 10, 38, 40, 43, 50
Rinns of Islay 15, 20, 35, 36, 37
Robert Burns 9
Robert Louis Stevenson 19, 23, 38
Robert Stevenson 19, 20, 21, 24, 28, 30, 36, 55, 56, 75, 78, 82, 88
Robert the Bruce 9, 10, 27
Rona 15, 22, 42
Roosts 67
Ross 13, 15, 25, 36, 38, 51, 53
Rubh' Re 11, 17, 23, 53, 54
Rubha nan Gall 15, 22, 42

S

Sanda 10, 15, 21, 32, 33, 34, 35
Scapa Flow 15, 67, 68, 69
Scott, Sir Walter 37
Scrabster 58, 59
Scurdie Ness 16, 22
Seven Hunters 49

Shags 30
Shetland 6, 11, 12, 15, 16, 17, 22, 25, 55, 69, 70, 72, 74, 75, 76
Sir Walter Scott 6, 9, 24, 25
Skerryvore 10, 15, 21, 22, 23, 37, 38, 55
Skervuile 16, 22
Sleat 42
Smith, Thomas 32, 61, 63
Solway 12
South Uist 15
Special Protection Area 55, 75
St Abb's Head 16, 22, 45
St Ninian's Isle 75
Start Point 14, 20, 63
Stenness 72
Stevenson 6, 13, 19, 20, 21, 22, 23, 24, 25, 26, 28, 30, 33, 36, 37, 38, 40, 41, 42, 44, 45,
    49, 51, 52, 53, 55, 56, 58, 63, 66, 67, 70, 71, 72, 75, 77, 78, 79, 80, 81, 82, 88
        Alan 33, 38, 41, 51, 67
        David 26, 41, 42, 44, 52, 53, 58, 63, 70, 71
        David A. 38, 40, 49, 66, 72, 77, 81
        Family 72
        Robert 28, 30, 36, 55, 56, 75, 78, 82, 88
        Robert Louis 38
        Thomas 26, 42, 52, 63, 71
        Stevenson family 6, 13, 19, 23, 72
Stoer Head 11, 16, 22, 52
Stornoway 15
Stranraer 10, 28, 29
Strathy Point 17
Stroma 16, 23, 59
Stronsay 16
Sule Skerry 16, 23
Sumburgh 12, 15, 20, 74, 75, 76

T

Tarbat Ness 15, 20, 55, 56
Tay 12, 78
Thomas Smith 13, 19, 20, 24, 32, 61, 63
Thomas Stevenson 22, 23, 24, 26, 42, 52, 63
Thurso 11, 58, 59
Tiree 10, 15, 21, 37, 38
Tiumpan Head 16, 23
Tod Head 16, 23
Trinity House 13, 23, 33, 37, 46, 70, 79
Turnberry 10, 16, 22, 26, 27

U

Unst 15, 22, 70, 71, 72
Ushenish 15, 22, 40, 42

V

Viking 10, 11, 29, 50, 76

W

Western Isles 10, 50
Westray 11, 16, 64, 67
Wick 15, 18, 19, 38, 62, 84, 87
World War Two 28, 54, 59, 62, 68, 78, 80, 81, 83

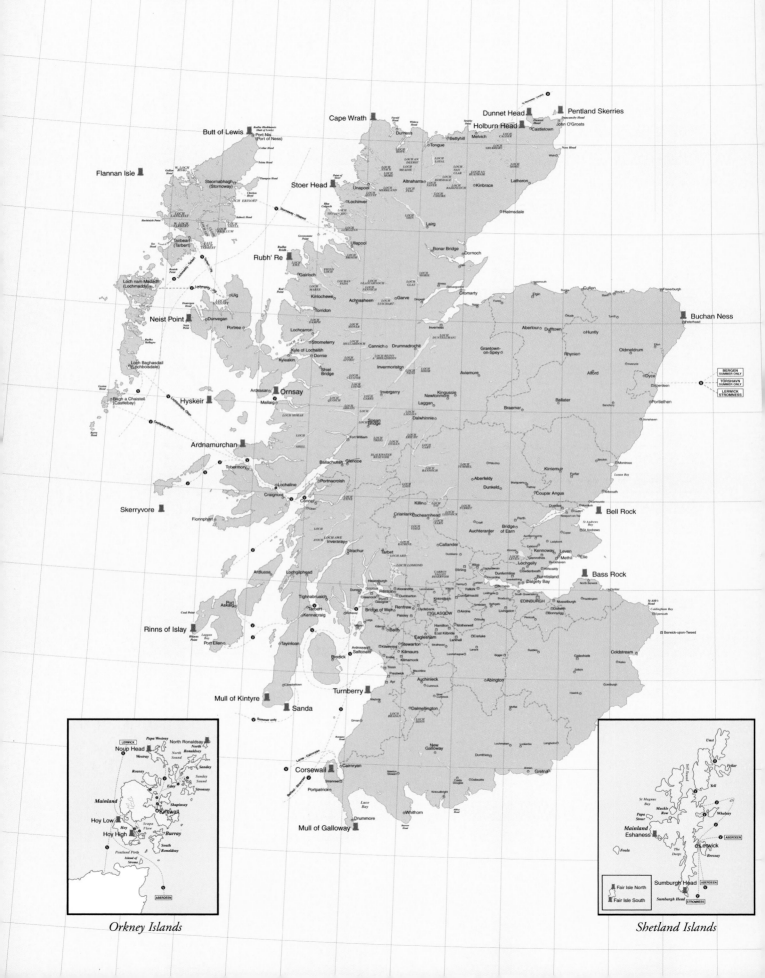

Orkney Islands

Shetland Islands